The Small Business Start-Up Workbook

– A Step-By-Step Guide to Successful Small Business Ownership

Mark A. Torr BSA, CPB, CPC, RTRP

To purchase books in quantity for corporate or academic use or as part of an incentive program, please email info@blackbullaccounting.com.

Copyright © 2014 by **BlackBull Learning, Inc.**

ALL RIGHTS RESERVED. No part of this book may be reproduced or transmitted in any form by any means, electronic or mechanical, including photocopying and recording, or by any information storage and retrieval system, except as may be expressly permitted in writing from the publisher. Requests for permission should be addressed to BlackBull Learning, Inc., Attn: Rights and Permissions Department, 6965 El Camino Real #105-110, Carlsbad, CA 92009.

Editorial Director: Tiffany Torr – BSA, EA
Project Editor: Linda Black
Printed by: CreateSpace
Published by: BlackBull Learning, Inc.
Cover Design: Nicole Slauson Designs (www.nicoleslauson.com)
Photography: Tehara Tweed Photography (www.teharatweed.com)

Library of Congress Cataloging-in-Publication Data is available on file.

ISBN-13: 978-1503238626
ISBN-10: 1503238628

Printed in the United States of America

This book's purpose is to provide accurate and authoritative information on the topics covered. It is sold with the understanding that neither the author nor the publisher is using this book to render legal, financial, accounting, and other professional services or advice. BlackBull Learning, Inc., BlackBull Accounting, Inc., and the author assume no liability resulting from action taken based on the information included herein. Mention of a company name does not constitute endorsement.

DEDICATION

America rose to greatness through the efforts of visionaries, hard workers, and risk takers. The greatest achievers in history created their legacies. They did not wait for opportunity to come seek them. This book salutes all hard workers and visionaries, foreign and domestic, whose minds dream with the same inspiration of those who came before them. For those unique people, they still believe opportunity is everywhere. It just takes a special set of eyeglasses to see it. I applaud each and every individual who puts on those glasses and looks to the horizon. From the corner lemonade stand to the multi-national conglomerate, every business starts as a vision. These people, the entrepreneurs and small business owners, believe and trust that a better life resides just over the horizon. Such faith and determination deserves to be honored, respected, and replicated.

This book is dedicated to my amazing and talented wife and business partner Tiffany, our four amazing children, Dalton, Austin, Tristan, and Sophia, and to all the courageous men and women who have started, or have decided to start, their own business ventures. As a business owner, I feel that I have discovered one of life's greatest secrets. Business ownership is the very embodiment of the American Dream. I hope this book helps you dream big and helps make those dreams come true.

Mark A. Torr

TABLE OF CONTENTS

Acknowledgments xi

Foreword xiii

Introduction xvii

1 Is starting a small business right for you? 1
You may already be a small business owner 1
Why starting a small business seems to be the answer for many 3
Why do you feel a small business is right for you? 5
Are you a self-starter? 6
Do you need to be managed or are you driven? 7
Be honest about your character traits and skill sets 7
Are there family members to consider? 8
Little stuff matters 9
Can you afford it? Can you afford _not_ trying? 11
Can you make your new business a priority? 13
Are you willing and able to quit your day job? 14

2 Things to ponder before jumping in with both feet 17
How to make good decisions 17
What business is right for you? 22
What does your business look like in your head and on paper? ... 27
Where do you see yourself in the near and distant future? 29
What services will you offer, how, and why? 30
Are you starting from scratch or taking over an existing business? ... 33

3 The Business Plan 37
What is a business plan and do you need one? 37
Where can you get help? 39
The main topics to consider 40

Executive Summary	40
Management	42
Services Provided	47
Marketing	51
Finances	59

4 Who do you want to be when you grow up? 67

Deciding on the name of your company	67
What services will you provide or refuse to provide?	77
Performing a name search	78
Filing for your Fictitious Business Name (FBN)	79
Choosing a business entity	81
Setting up your S-Corporation or LLC	87
Applying for your Employer Identification Number (EIN)	88
Applying for your business license	89
Do you need a sales tax license, use tax account, or seller's permit?	90
Setting up your business checking account	91
Securing your business credit and debit cards	94
Creating your marketing and collateral materials	95
Logo	95
Business Cards	100
Collateral Materials and Products	102

5 It's time to set up your home office 105

How should you design your home office?	105
Where is the best place to set it up?	109
Choosing your furniture, fixtures, and tools	110
Desks, chairs, tables, and credenza/hutch	111
File cabinets	112
Lighting and fans	112
Shelving and storage	113
Other important items	114

	Computer, software, and hardware	115
	What if you outgrow your home office?	125
6	**Marketing your brand and finding your clients**	**127**
	Stay true to your brand	127
	Focus on the clients you want, not the clients you need	128
	Fishing for clients	129
	Finding your niche	130
	Customizing your services	131
	Find mailing lists	132
	Asking for referrals	133
	Presentations and organizations	135
7	**Creating your website and tapping social media**	**139**
	The benefits of having a business website	139
	How to get your website off the ground	141
	Do you need to register your website with search engines?	144
	Search Engine Optimization (SEO)	145
	Portals and file sharing	146
	What about all that other stuff?	148
	Built-in content	148
	Monthly newsletters	149
	Blogging	149
	Calculators	150
	Web-links	151
	Web 2.0, social media, and social networks	152
	LinkedIn	153
	Facebook, Twitter, and YouTube	154
	Professional organizations, groups, and forums	155
8	**Can you afford all of this?**	**159**
	Start-Up costs	160

What rates should you charge?	160
Should you use a loss leader in your billing and pricing practice?	161
How should you collect your fees and accounts receivable?	167
Tracking your time and mileage	170
Creating and managing a budget	171
Create expense accounts	172
Review on a regular basis	174
Set up your bookkeeping	175
Organize your source documents	177

9 Best Practices and Efficiencies — 179

Six Sigma	179
The six sigma philosophy	180
Best practices	182
How to find your "sweet spot"	184
Benchmarking	184
Standards	184
Management	184
Employees	186
Operations	187
Sales and Marketing	188
Innovation	189
Information Technology (IT)	190
Making changes	191
Client Contracts, Agreements, and Letters of Engagement	194
Policies, Terms of Use, Disclosures, and Disclaimers	194
Fine print	195
Two wrongs don't make a right	196
File maintenance and security	197
Filing Baskets	198
Digital Files	198
File Storage	199

Conclusion	202
Appendices	205
Notes	227
References	229
About the author	233
Index	237

Mark A. Torr

ACKNOWLEDGMENTS

My road traveled as a small business owner is lined with hundreds of people I have thanked and continue to thank along the way. From family, to friends, to professors, to pastors, to colleagues, to professionals, and even my own clients, all have made contributions which have helped shape me and my businesses. While I have proactively collected valuable training, coaching, and input in order to make good decisions, some amazing ideas and input have come to me by pure accident or coincidence. I am thankful for the ability to distill bad input from good, for the humility to admit when I am wrong, and the flexibility to change direction.

As is often the case, time spent with the business usually means time away from the wife and kids. It is a delicate balance. I want to apologize for the times I was not there to attend a soccer game, robot competition, or family dinner. I also want to thank my wife and kids for the amazing understanding and support they have shown me. Our dinner conversations often involve business, politics, and economics. When not rolling their eyes, my family participates in our dinner chats. I believe it was during one of our dinner debates where I was finally challenged to write this book. I hope it is received with more than just exaggerated eye rolls.

Mark A. Torr

FOREWORD

Toward the end of 2012 I lost my job unexpectedly only three months after relocating to a new state. As an expert on the job search process for transitioning Veterans and building companywide initiatives around hiring, there were limited opportunities in the small business environment of San Diego, CA. The expertise I had was unique, with less than a handful of people with my skillset and background. I found myself deciding to make the best out of a challenging situation and establish a consulting company.

Starting a business is a daunting task, regardless of your previous experience, or any amount of education. I've spent the majority of my adult life in some form of educational pursuit: a Bachelor's degree in Psychology (BS), most of a Masters in Community Psychology (MS), a Masters of Science in Management (MS), and finally finishing eleven plus years of college with a doctorate (EdD) in Organizational Leadership. As a Marine Corps officer for 10 years I traveled the world, ran exercises in foreign countries and completed a tour in Iraq. In the corporate world I've worked at a medium sized start up, a small, well-established company and the tech-retail giant, Amazon. Starting a business levels the playing field for everyone. Education and experience is great to have in your toolkit, but alphabet soup after your name doesn't guarantee to make you successful at it.

Having lofty credentials often create a false sense of security and confidence for would-be business owners. Accomplished individuals often times end up learning the hard way that college courses are not adequate to prep a person for the world of business ownership. Mistakes are extremely costly. Time, money, and opportunities are lost. There are things business owners need to know that 11 years of school and 15 years of being a professional did not or could not teach me. I still think starting my own business was the most challenging endeavor of all. I made numerous mistakes at the start, often costing me time and money (also known as – the only two things that matter as a business owner!).

A number of resources exist to help you get navigate and understand the process, many offering opportunities at your pace and learning style. Companies can quickly help you establish your business for a fee while continuing to charge you for every piece of advice and resource. If you're constrained by time or unwilling to learn the process (like me), you can opt for paying to receive these services and advice. However, none of these companies will help you evaluate whether or not you're prepared to make the jump and become self-employed.

Regardless of the type of business you establish, there is one area no one wants to get wrong- finances. Navigating the financial implications of owning a business is an art form, and having an accountant you can trust who also looks out for your best interest is essential as an entrepreneur. When I first met Mark and the BlackBull Accounting family I knew I was embarking on the right track with the best possible resource for my business. Our conversations are often humorous, and even serious situations turn entertaining. On many occasions these optimistic discussions allowed me to see a tiny spark of hope during stressful times. Mark always focuses on providing me with the best possible guidance to meet my needs, no matter what situations we face.

When you're feeling alone on the island of small business ownership it helps to have a trusted ally. Mark has consistently steered me in the right direction over the past two years. His guidance was critical in the beginning as I set up my business banking accounts and learned more about taxes for business owners. I feel confident knowing he has my best interest at heart and is willing to help educate me in the process. His book includes the fun and engaging personality I've come to enjoy working with. It's easy to sink into, as he writes with the demeanor of having a casual conversation with you. He is open and honest and includes a number of realistic examples while also being extremely comprehensive about the multitude of things you may not have considered for your business. The information provided is invaluable, and I encourage you to take the time to answer the questions honestly so you make a well-informed decision about whether or not starting a business is the right choice for your situation.

At the end of the day starting a business is never easy. Knowing what you want to achieve in the long run is critical to making it through the rough days. Being prepared by knowing what to expect will help you navigate sudden land mines. Education and experience are good things, but don't underestimate the power and effectiveness of hard work when blended with common sense and good advice. Having access to the right resources and advice to guide you along the way will help you maintain your sanity on the road to success. The Small Business Start-Up Workbook is a great place to help you prepare for the nuances of business ownership and decide if becoming an entrepreneur is your next move.

Wishing you the best of luck,

Lisa Parrott

Dr. Lisa M. Parrott
Career DI

Mark A. Torr

INTRODUCTION

Dear (future) Business Owner,

    As a long-time business owner and economic fanatic, it only makes sense that I finally sat my rear end down at my computer to formally create a How-To Guide for starting a business. The idea of writing this book initially came to me about ten years ago. It sounded like a novel idea, but I laughed it off. The idea came to me again about five years ago based on client requests. I created a condensed bullet point cheat sheet as a stopgap measure. Then, about three years ago, my clients' demand for small business coaching and personal record keeping was impossible to ignore. To address the issue, I created an expanded, five-page, step-by-step, how-to guide to starting a business. This small guide worked... well, sort of worked. All the information was accurate and helpful, but it was surgical in nature. There was no broad-brush approach. I wrote it as if I was the one using it. As it turns out, it was not a very effective tool for my new, start-up business owners. They wanted a more whole-istic approach to business ownership, one that explained the **philosophy** and not just the **mechanics**. I needed to find a solution.

    To address the issue I began coaching clients. I held their hands, listened to their concerns, and walked them through the process. I loved it; they loved it. I still love it, but when running a business and striving for efficiencies, the one-on-one model I was using began to create constraints. The demands of tax season do not afford me the luxury of one-on-one coaching for the first four months of the year. Not only that, but sometimes I wonder if I am really helping my clients by just talking to them.

I did not realize that the lecture-format does not work for everyone until my career began to require a significant amount of public speaking. I love public speaking, especially to large groups. However, if my presentations went too long, I could see audience members start to get restless. I would hear a voice in my head warn me, "You are going to lose them!" I would start to feel like the teacher in the old *Peanuts* cartoons. Do you remember the sound of the teacher's voice? "Whaawaa waawan waaaaaw wah wa waaaaan." I felt like I needed to stop talking and back away from the mic. But wait, didn't the audience come to hear me speak? Well then, why were their eyes starting to glass over? It really threw me off my rhythm. I learned that while the lecture format is awesome, many people do not respond well to it. They start to feel like they are back in school waiting for the recess bell to ring. This is another reason a book seems to makes so much sense. The words coming off the page don't make a sound! Many people prefer a physical book, a pen in hand, and taking notes to a lecture. Now my clients can read this book, save me hours of lecturing, and no one requires smelling salts at the end. Bingo! Another win-win scenario.

There is another reason I finally created this book. It is a much better value for my clients. It is wise to grab some cheap knowledge before gaining expensive experience. I found that, to really ramp-up, a new business owner required a minimum of 3 - 5 days of my time. At $65 per hour and up, my clients were out $1,500 - $3,000 and were still calling me with questions. Here lies another constraint or dilemma. For $1,500, I felt obligated to answer additional questions at no cost, but also knew I should be charging for my time. I also discovered the effectiveness of my coaching was in direct correlation to the learning styles of my clients. The results were subjective. Were they good listeners? Did they take good notes? Did they have questions prepared in advance? Did the coaching trigger more questions down the road? If I was only concerned with revenues for my company, I would just keep things as-is; coach and bill, coach and bill. But this dynamic goes against everything I stand for when it comes to value, efficiency, effectiveness, and service.

Now, with the book, I feel like I have a bunch of Mini-Mes out there doing all the coaching for me. The book is always available, reminds clients of what they need to do, alleviates the need to take notes, doesn't bill for its time, and works seven days a week. Then, when clients want follow-up consultations, they are in and out in an hour or two and off to the races. My clients get what they need, save a bunch of money, and I only have to hear myself speak for an hour or so. Perfect.

I also want to give you a heads-up. There are plenty of books currently on the market to assist the small business owner. Some are good, some are not. Many books on the market claim to be for the "start-up" business owner but then overwhelm and/or confuse a new business owner with too much information. I have read other "start-up" books on the market which include chapters on Business Negotiations, Inventory Control, Consumer Credit, Mailing Systems, Accounting, Bookkeeping, Legal Representation, Hiring Processes, Selling Techniques, Finances, and the like. These, in my opinion, are stand-alone subjects that require their own book(s), training, and/or courses to successfully learn or grasp the concepts. Skimming a few pages of a start-up book should not dictate the decisions of a business owner on these critical topics. I would urge you to hire a professional to address such issues, immerse yourself in research, attend college courses, or all the above.

This book is designed to thoroughly equip you to launch and run a successful business. As your business grows, you may or may not need to invest time and money into further learning and advanced skill sets. What this book does <u>not</u> do is try to impress you with a few hundred pages of information which will not contribute to your success. My goal is not trying to impress you with everything I know. This book is a portion of what I know; it is the portion I believe you will need and appreciate when making the decision to start your own small business. I have worked very hard to keep this book direct, pertinent, and valuable. I believe it is enough and not too much. I hope you agree.

Best wishes,

Mark A. Torr – Owner, BlackBull Accounting, Inc.

Note: Go grab your pencil and highlighter. This is workbook. I want its readers to not only READ, but also DO. You will be asked to complete questions and surveys in the Appendix as the book rolls along. This book will document your answers and serve as a reference tool for you during the life of your new business. Now get reading and have some fun.

Chapter 1

Is starting a small business right for you?

The Small Business Start-Up Workbook is designed to provide support, suggestions, and guidance to our brave, hard-working, forward-thinking tax payers who are trying to better themselves and their families. The decision to step forward into the world of the small business owner is not one which comes easily for most. It is a very special breed of person who ventures out to pioneer new opportunities. The odyssey of the small business owner involves risk, sacrifice, stress, and uncertainty. This exciting quest requires vision and a positive outlook. It requires one to see opportunity and potential beyond the limitations and obvious challenges staring them right in the face. I salute the brave business people who make this decision. Kudos to you for taking the first step.

You may already be a small business owner

You may be a small business owner and not even realize it! Did you know the small business world includes those involved in direct sales, multi-level marketing (MLM), independent contracting, charities, non-profit activities, hobbyists, and those simply trying to run their homes more efficiently? Even rental property ownership is considered a small business venture. At tax time each year, I am surprised by how many taxpayers do not know that are actually small business owners. These discoveries are made through a series of questions that I ask my clients. The answers they provide reveal they have been operating a small business for some time without ever taking the formal steps to make the business official. I have even had the IRS inform my clients they are business owners after incorrectly filing only a personal tax return.

Would you like me to give you a few real-world examples from this last tax season? I have quite a few. The six listed here work well to make my point.

- **Photographer**- A new client of mine has been operating a photography "hobby" in which she is quite active, has substantial expenses, and is generating income. She was unaware of the tax advantages that including her photography in her personal tax return would provide. She is now officially a small business owner.

- **Multi-Level Marketing**- A few of my new tax and bookkeeping clients have been involved in direct and/or multi-level marketing sales. Arbonne, Essential Oils, Amway, Herbalife, Juice Plus, Shaklee, Beach Body, Legal Shield, NuSkin, Monavie, Melaluca, etc. are all small business ventures and need to be treated as such.

- **Mechanic**- A new client of mine has been repairing cars on the side to make a few bucks, but he was losing thousands of dollars in unrealized tax benefits from not making his auto repair business official. We fixed that.

- **Ammunition Reloading**- I discovered one of my clients has been having ammunition reloading parties in his basement with his active-duty military buddies. We made his business official. He now enjoys all the tax benefits.

- **Homemaker**- Did you know being a "homemaker" is an occupation in the eyes of the IRS? Operating a home is like operating a small business. Money is exchanged every day. There is much which needs to be managed. Clients come to me to help organize and run their homes. If the home is not running efficiently, the family suffers.

- **Daycare / Babysitting / Pet sitting**- These vocations are extremely common. A military mom client of mine was watching a couple of her friend's children on base as a favor. Her reputation grew as did the number of children being dropped off at her house. Before she knew it, she was watching over 20 children and earning much more money than her husband. The same goes for a pet sitter I know. What started as a fun gesture to a neighbor turned into a solid business for her. This young lady earned enough to purchase a nice car and put herself through college.

It is common for a taxpayer to assume their "hobby" activity is not a small business for a variety of reasons- it is not what they do full-time, the activity does not produce much income, or they do not have a business license. Like the client examples listed here, there is a chance you may be closer to small business ownership than you think. All businesses start out as ideas and many sprout up from hobbies which then grow into impressive businesses. Never underestimate the potential of a good idea.

Why starting a small business seems to be the answer for many

If you are like me, being a small business owner was something I dreamt about starting at age 10. Like any other kid, I wanted things, lots of things. But I didn't have any money and my guardians (my parents both died when I was seven years old) didn't have anything for me beyond my $5 a week allowance. So, I was stuck.

Each week I would pour over my Bass Pro Shops catalog and walk through the sporting goods departments at Sears, Gemco (yes, I'm that old), Fedco (don't laugh), and Kmart. I would touch just about every fishing pole, fishing lure, tackle box, baseball glove, BMX bike, and beach cruiser. I would try to ignore the price tag until the last possible minute because I knew the tag would kill my dream and good mood. Paying $6.00 for a fishing lure 35 years ago was a fortune. (Have you calculated my age yet?) I clearly had a problem which needed a solution. That solution came to me one Saturday morning when I was watching cartoons.

To be honest, I can't take all the credit for my small business owner epiphany. It was about 9:30 that Saturday morning when my older brother came downstairs and started to give me a hard time. He said those things a 10 year old kid hates to hear. "It's a beautiful day outside," "You shouldn't be wasting your time on cartoons," "Why don't you go play outside?" I just wanted him to leave me alone so I could try to understand what *Snagglepuss* was trying to say. We argued back and forth for a few minutes. I complained that my bike was broken, I needed a new one, but couldn't afford one. His response was, "Well, go work and make some money." He might as well have said, "If you jump really hard, you can land on the moon." It seemed that ridiculous to a ten-year-old. My inner voice pressed me, however, and I made him explain what he meant.

My brother suggested that I go wash windows, wash cars, or mow lawns. Well, I knew how to wash cars (or had the confidence to act like I could) so I figured it was worth a shot. I went to the garage, grabbed my red wagon, and filled it with a bucket, sponges, brushes, soap, Windex, rags, and the hose from the front yard. Then I started banging on my neighbors' doors." The kid with big glasses and a bad haircut was going for it. What happened within the next two hours completely blew my mind!

To make a long story short, in two hours I had earned $40 cash and had a route of five homes of people who all wanted their cars washed every weekend. I didn't even make it half way around my street. Of the eight homes I knocked on, I think five wanted my help. I even had families leave cash for me under their doormats with the cars in the driveway when they were still asleep or not home. I was a kid with crushed dreams one minute, but two hours later, I was knocking down $20 per hour, tax free, at age ten. I still get chills when I think about that Saturday. It was so empowering, so liberating. Since that day I have been 100% invested in the small business ownership philosophy. That's where it's at, baby!

Now, fast forward to 2014. The economy is on life support, unemployment is at 20% (using true economic indicators), and people with college degrees are working at Starbucks and Target to make ends meet. Many people have serious levels of education, experience, and skill sets but the marketplace simply doesn't have enough jobs to go around. This is why so many talented people are creating their own business. If they can't find a job, they will create their own. And it's working.

Why do you feel a small business is right for you?

Are you tired of your boss? Tired of following rules you don't agree with? Tired of the politics? Tired of the commute? Tired of being unemployed? Tired of low wages? Tired of the gossip? Tired of the cubicles? Tired of being more qualified yet under-paid? Tired of being away from your family? Tired of the travel? Tired of the repetition? Tired of being downsized? What is it that you really want and what are you willing to risk to get it?

For me, looking like an idiot pulling a red wagon from door to door was worth the risk. Starting a small business is worth the risk for millions of

Americans, but it's not for everyone. If you are naturally outgoing, a leader, make friends easily, have some confidence, and don't have a fear of crowds or public speaking, then being a small business owner might be a good fit (Note - public speaking may not be part of your business model; it's just a positive character indicator). On the other hand, if the opposite is true of you, it doesn't mean that business ownership is not for you. It just means your uphill climb could be a bit steeper. Starting a small business requires a healthy combination of guts, motivation, skill, determination, savvy, character, morals, and ethics. Are you ready to walk away from the paid sick days, the holiday pay, the health insurance, and the break room snacks? Do you still feel this is the right path for you? Ok, then let's get into it.

Are you a self-starter?

I certainly hope so. I have heard many clients of mine over the years complain about how they are micromanaged at work. They hate it. But what if that structure and oversight was suddenly gone? How would that person perform in a management-free environment? Many people spin out of control, crash, and burn when they don't receive constant direction and input. You need to be realistic before making the decision to start your own company.

Winston Churchill said, **"The world is run by tired men"**. You will soon find out how true this statement is. Owning a company doesn't mean sleeping in until 9:00, watching TV and eating Frosted Flakes until 12:00, working from 12:00 to 3:00, and then shutting everything down to go to hit a twilight round at the local municipal course. It's quite the opposite. For the first 2 or 3 years, 12 hour workdays are all too common. Yes, you need to block some down time to recover, but you should get used to energy bars and jars of mixed nuts during the ramp up. Owning a business is a long-term payoff. The time for coasting comes years down the road. It takes serious motivation to get there, but trust me, it is well worth it!

Do you need to be managed or are you driven?

People and businesses need to be managed, but they don't necessarily require bosses to do that. At BlackBull, we are managed by our calendar. We block schedule everything! Every task we have, every appointment, every to-do, every reminder, every exam, every required office function; it all goes into our calendar. We use Microsoft Outlook and sync it with our Google calendar. Every morning begins with a review of the calendar. We wake up, open the calendar in our phones, and learn what is scheduled that day. Yes, we are driven, but it almost feels like our calendar is pushing us from behind. We are being told what to do without someone actually in our faces. It works brilliantly. We don't stop working until everything on our list that day is complete or rescheduled to another day. We know the next day is going to bring us another long list of tasks to accomplish.

The point here is to use the tools around you to help you stay motivated. Brilliant people have developed brilliant software and apps to help us along the way. Heck, we even use an old-fashioned picture calendar. It hangs on the wall. Do yourself a favor and use good tools. We will get into specific tools, software, and apps in Chapter 5.

Be honest about your character traits and skill sets

When I was 15 years into business ownership and doing well, I still had room to learn a very valuable lesson. An attorney friend/colleague of mine turned me on to a book called **StrengthsFinder 2.0**. I highly recommend this book for all business owners (http://www.strengthsfinder.com/home.aspx). Our society tends to demonize those with very powerful business attributes. For example, an extremely organized person is labeled "anal retentive." Hard workers are called "over-achievers" or "workaholics." Tech savvy individuals are called "dorks," "geeks," or "nerds." You get the point. Those with employee mindsets tend to avoid those who demonstrate such characteristics, but as a business owner, you will soon learn to embrace the people with those monikers. A business owner sees those character "flaws" as powerful business attributes. You will end up hiring those people; not gossiping about them. I needed an office manager a few years back and hired the most uptight and anal retentive person I could find. She was a rock star for me from day one!

The point here, don't try to be someone you are not. Figure out what your strengths are, embrace them, and exploit them. Once you know who you are NOT, hire or get help from someone who IS that person.

Running a business takes discipline. If you are a late sleeper, set your alarm. If you are a vampire, try to get to bed earlier. If you have doubts, read self-help books. If you can't focus, create a schedule. Use available tools to keep you moving forward. Once you have good momentum, don't let it stop. Redirect that momentum into being highly productive. Maximize your strengths while minimizing your weaknesses.

Are there family members to consider?

Ah yes, the family. This can get tricky. There is really no perfect scenario here. Family members can help or hinder. Perhaps you are starting a company to provide for your family and create flexibility in your schedule to be with them. Perhaps it's because you do not have much family that you are afforded the opportunity to start a business. Is a spouse encouraging you and pushing you from behind or getting in your way and holding you back? The same can be asked of your children.

If there is family involved, I strongly suggest having a team meeting to explain your goals and plans. Have everybody get on board and help in every way possible. Believe me, there will be sacrifices made, which the family will feel, while energy is being redirected in to the business. Meals, soccer games, homework help, and movie nights will be missed. The house will get messy, lawns will grow tall, pictures will remain unhung, and cars will remain dirty. Family members will need to pick up the slack when you need the help.

I have four children. Even though I have been doing this for quite a while, I still have family meetings before I take more college courses, go out of town, or ramp up for another tax season. Tax season is crazy on a family. I turn into a ghost and am rarely seen. I can do very little outside of my responsibilities at BlackBull. The family agrees to a plan of action before every tax season so we can all make it through. Vacations, movies, beach runs, golf, tennis, family dinners, help with homework, etc. all gets put on hold for four months. That's the deal. At the same time, I need to be hyper-efficient in everything I do so I am not wasting one more minute away from my family than is absolutely necessary. Time management is very important.

Little stuff matters

When starting a business, you are now in the public arena. Actions have consequences, both positive and negative. You will want to pause and think twice about the actions you take. In the normal course of a day, we cut corners all the time. We leave the dishes in the sink, let the empty trash cans sit on the curb too long, allow the car to remain dirty, and let emails and voicemails sit too long before answering them. When your company brand is at stake, a new level of vigilance needs to be part of your business model. The little stuff now matters.

It will be wise to get into the habit of keeping your promise on the little things. For many, this takes adjustment. You will need to make sure your yes means Yes and your no means No. Do what you say you will do. Do not compromise. If you get into the habit of not keeping your word on small stuff, you may not keep your word on big stuff. Not a good habit. The success of your brand will depend on your word and your consistency.

Quick story: I had a scheduled appointment with a client at my office. She was supposed to drop off some basic paperwork for an amendment on her tax return. I was delayed in the field and did not make it back to my office on time. She arrived on time, rang the doorbell with no answer, and then left a voicemail after she could not reach me. After waiting for me for fifteen minutes, she returned home. I was unable to take her call in the field so I returned her call when I made it back to the office. I apologized for being delayed. She was very understanding and not upset at all. I was surprised. Then, she asked if she should head back over to my office. I could not believe she was willing to come back after I missed our appointment. I was faced with the following multiple choices:

A) Do I make her drive back over?
B) Do I make a house-call and head over to her residence?
C) Do I book another appointment for her to drop her stuff off later?
D) Do I have her mail, fax, or upload her documents?

The easy thing to do is A), have her drive back over. After all, I am a professional. I'm a busy guy. Professionals make their clients wait all the time. She had no problem returning to the office. She expected to anyway.

However, I chose B). I know that I caused the problem. I did not hold up my end of the arrangement, so I felt it was my duty to make the situation right. I drove to my client's home and consulted with her for an hour. As it turns out, we did not need to amend her return. She simply needed a consultation. She asked to pay for my time. Knowing I caused this problem to begin with, I did not charge her for my time or accept any money. She was amazed. In return, she referred her neighbor to me before I could leave her home. I do my best to remember that the little stuff matters in business. It was a challenge, but I felt it was the right thing to do.

Can you afford it? Can you afford <u>not</u> trying?

Like an old western movie, there needs to be a "reckoning" before taking on a new business. Do you have the time and money to pull this off? Or is it because you don't have the time and money that you need to pull this off? Either position is fine, but you need to have a clear understanding of the position you are in. Starting a new business may deplete your resources- time, money, assets, energy, patience, etc. However, if done correctly, it should also replenish those resources as you go. At the end of year one, if you break even, you are probably on a good road and should continue the journey. Year two should produce modest results. Year three should see some legitimate income, and by year four, you should be able to fully replace the income you left behind at your old job. Of course, these are general benchmarks, but they provide a point of comparison to gauge your progress. But remember, income is not the only barometer for measurement. Some people choose to start their own business knowing they may earn less money, but gain the quality of life they desire.

Start-up expenses directly correlate to the type of business you are opening and the level of service you intend to provide. A massage therapist can be up and running after only shelling out a few hundred dollars for a massage table, linens, oils, some business cards, and a spare bedroom (when not mobile). Mechanics, on the other hand, require thousands of dollars in tools before they can even work on their first car. Then, workspace is needed on top of that.

Take a good look at your assets to determine your starting point. Do you have $500 cash at your disposal or $50,000? Even if you have wads of cash and nothing but time, I still recommend starting small and letting your business grow organically. Mistakes will be made along the way. Mistakes cost money! It is better to make small mistakes as you go so the lessons are relatively inexpensive. That way, you avoid expensive lessons down the road. The same holds true when purchasing an existing business. You will still want to let that new business marinate for a few years as you learn your craft before making decisions which can backfire, cost you valuable resources, or put you out of business altogether.

Business owners are dreamers and visionaries. This acts like a double-edge sword. The same moxie which gets a business off the ground is the same moxie which can become reckless, uncalculated, and can bring that business crashing down. Be smart enough to know your strengths and limitations. The brains you know you don't have, you need to borrow. Surround yourself with wise people and hire professionals to do what you are not able to execute <u>skillfully</u> yourself. BlackBull does the accounting and taxes for many brilliant and accomplished individuals and businesses, because bookkeeping and tax preparation are NOT our clients' specialties. They pay BlackBull a few bucks to make their headaches disappear. This frees them up to do what they are good at. Smart business owners quickly realize their limitations and delegate whenever possible.

The good news is, you can grow into your goals. A client of mine, a massage therapist, started cheap, small, and mobile. She worked out of the trunk of her car and built a solid client base over a few years. Once her income and client base was at a desired level, she opened a small studio store front. When she outgrows the small studio, she can get a bigger space, and so on. The same holds true for the mechanic, the accountant, the golf pro, or the restaurateur. Remember, how does a person eat an entire elephant? One bite at a time.

Can you make your new business a priority?

Each business owner will eventually reach a fork in the road. There comes a point to jump in with both feet or to go sit back down. This "pee or get off the pot" moment is extremely obvious for some, yet cloudy and obscured for others.

For some, the decision is made for them. They get laid-off, fired, or downsized from their cushy job. What if the same happened to their spouse? Some people choose to start a business while others are forced into it. Either way, for that new business to succeed, it requires a 100% commitment. That level of commitment often times seems to correlate with the level of desperation or discomfort in which the new business owners find themselves.

For instance, how hard is a husband going to work at his yard maintenance business if his doctor wife is earning $300,000 a year? And how hard will a wife work at her Arbonne business when her husband is earning $250,000 as a regional sales manager? A business owner needs to be highly motivated to be highly successful. Good fortune does not fall into a person's lap while watching Oprah. Good fortune is earned by people who want something bad enough.

Are you willing and able to quit your day job?

It might be difficult for a person to quit a job earning $40,000 a year with benefits. The level of dissatisfaction must be very high to cause a person to leave such comfort. Perhaps the problem is caused by a family illness, a decision to relocate, or by being grossly underpaid. Imagine how difficult it would be for a firefighter to leave a job earning $60,000 a year, with benefits, working only two weeks a month. The payoff to leave that position must be extremely high.

The good news here is that it doesn't necessarily have to be an All-or-Nothing proposition. Most firefighters I know occupy their free time with a side business. One pours concrete slabs, another has a tree trimming business while another has a pool cleaning route. This is possible only because the firefighter has time on his or her hands. For most employees, they are obligated to a 40 hour work week at a minimum. Mix in the commuting, kids, and errands and there is barely enough time left to watch an old episode of *Survivor* on the DVR.

The best way to approach such a jumping-off point is by creating a cost analysis or pros vs. cons list and rate the value of being an employee vs. being a business owner. Here is a chart I created to help you start mapping out your decision.

Put an "X" to mark how you feel in each Yes or No box for both the Employee and Business Owner columns.

(Go to Appendices – Complete **Appendix A**)

	Employee		Business Owner	
	Yes	No	Yes	No
Convenient work hours				
Commuting / Traffic issues				
High cost of fuel or transportation				
High cost of wardrobe or uniforms				
Provides appropriate levels of income				
Provides structured lunches or breaks				
Overtime pay availability				
Paid holidays				
Paid sick days				
Insurance benefits				
High levels of stress and responsibility				
Professional support / back office available				
Obligation to clients				
Workplace, furniture, and tools				
Provides education and training				
Maximizes your skillset				
Room to achieve your potential				
Power to make decisions				
Politics in the workplace				
Demands time away from family				
Conforms with 5, 10, 20 year plan				
Addresses retirement considerations				
Conforms with desired lifestyle				
Builds own self-worth				

Using this chart can help visualize the facts and remove many of the emotions from the decision-making process. In business, I tend to shy away from making decisions based on how I feel. I don't ignore my feelings, but they come secondary to the facts surrounding the decisions I need to make. After you complete the graph, count your Yes and your No votes. This is not the final determinant to starting a business, rather a good starting point.

Chapter 2

Things to ponder before jumping in with both feet

How to make good decisions

Before you get too far ahead of yourself, I want to spend a bit of time talking about the decision-making process. It will be extremely important for you to realize the potential impact the decisions you make will have on you, your business, and your family. Your entire life is the sum of the results of the decisions you make. I have made plenty of good decisions in my life and plenty of bad ones too. I have invested much to learn how to make good decisions and do my best to avoid making the bad ones. The funny thing is, I believe your mom, dad, or Sesame Street taught you some of these key tools when you were just a little kid.

I venture to guess that when you were little, your parents taught you to do what before crossing the street? Stop, drop, and roll? No, that was if you catch on fire. Climb under your desk? No, that was in the case of earthquakes. As kids, we were taught to stop, look, and listen, right? Kids are generally oblivious. I was no different. Before crossing the street, I was taught to stop, look both ways (twice), listen for cars, bikes or people, then proceed with caution. When you make decisions regarding your new business (and your life in general), you will want to practice what you learned as a kid. These days, it seems common for adults to abandon good decision-making and make poor decisions based on emotions, including guilt and fear. Don't do this.

Let me share some tried-and-true rules and secrets with you:

Rule #1: Determine if the decision is minor or major

Before making any decisions, you should look at your current dilemma, run it through a series of questions, and determine the gravity of the decision you need to make. There is quite a difference between purchasing liability insurance and purchasing a new coffee maker. The more significant the decision, the more care needs to go into it. To determine if a decision is major or minor, you can ask yourself the following questions:

1. **Is the decision you make going to be easily reversible?**
If yes, it's minor. If no, it's major.

2. **Is the decision you make going to be permanent?**
If yes, it's major. If no, it's most likely minor.

3. **Does this decision involve significant time, money, or effort?**
If yes, it's major. If no, it's most likely minor.

4. **What assumptions are you making regarding the issue?**
Minor or major, making assumptions raises a red flag. I will address this in just a bit.

5. **Do you know the difference between assumptions and facts?**
If no, get help. You should avoid making decisions based on assumptions. All decisions, big or small, should be based on fact. Become a lover of truth and fact. Assumptions can be landmines.

Note: Assumptions are not always dangerous, but they may be false. However, many assumptions may also be fact. For instance, I assume that the accounting industry has a going concern. I assume it will continue to exist because we have the IRS and GAAP. It is not probable that either of these will end in the near future. However, this is an assumption worth noting because in the event there is legislation to simplify the tax code, a removal of IRS regulation over tax preparers, or a flat tax is instituted, I will want to pay special attention so I am able to change my business model.

6. How much time will it take to gather your facts?
If little to no time, it's most likely minor. If much time is need to fact gather, it's major.

After crunching these six questions, you should have a better idea as to whether or not you are about to make a minor or major decision. Let's look at the ways to approach both. First, the minor decision.

Rule #2 – Making a minor decision
When it comes to making minor decisions, I recommend you do the following:

- **Spend an amount time fact finding relative to the scope of the decision**. Deciding on a stapler could take no time at all and be impulsive. Deciding on your coffee maker could involve a bit of online browsing or walking the isles at Target or Costco. Either way, the time and money investment is not very significant, just proportionate.

- **Have fun**. Don't turn your minor decisions into major ones. I believe you should enjoy the minor decision-making process. Shopping for a desk lamp or chair can be exciting when setting up your office. I actually enjoy shopping for office supplies. Try to smile when grabbing all of your office wares knowing you are setting your business up for success. Enjoy doing the small stuff. Major decisions can wear you out.

- **Be prepared to reverse your decision with no regrets.** Be able and willing to reverse your minor decisions when you discover they were poor. This is one reason you should use the minimum amount of time and effort when making minor decisions. Too much time spent on minor decisions can be tiresome, can deplete the energy you need for your major decisions, and creates a psychological fallacy causing you to think your minor decisions are now major. This is not a sunk cost. Misclassifying a minor decision into a major one makes reversal more difficult. Now, let's take a closer look at the major decision process.

Rule #3 – Making a major decision
When it comes to making major decisions, the process is much more involved. I recommend a four step process before "crossing the road" so you can safely make it safely to the other side.

Step 1 - Stop. Stop what you are doing, slow down, and sleep on it. Relax; take a breath. Major decisions cause our blood pressure, stress, and level of excitement to naturally rise. Watch out for an adrenalin rush. Being in this state is very bad for the decision making process. Remember, you will want to make decisions based on facts and not feelings. Make a solid effort to step back from the situation, delay if necessary, and regroup. In sales, the phrase is *"Time kills deals."* This is why salespeople want you to do the very opposite of what I just explained. Salespeople know that rushed decisions always go in their favor, not yours. An ancient proverb says *"By day they hear speech; by night they gain knowledge."*

Step 2 – Look. Look for the facts. Write the facts down, two columns, pros and cons. Respect the facts and let them guide you in your decisions making. Don't trust what you think; trust what you know. When fact finding, use many sources. Don't stop when you find a person or source which agrees with you. Collect as much data as possible so an educated and factual decision can be made. Seek the truth. Don't seek convenience. Don't cherry-pick facts which only support one position. Don't discriminate. Fact finding is a key tool to avoiding bad decisions and making great ones. Oh, you want another ancient proverb? How about the idiom *"Measure twice, cut once"* or *"Desire without knowledge is not good. Hasty feet miss the way."* I guess the second one here applies to Step 1 as well. Cool.

Step 3 – Listen. Listen to those around you. Surround yourself with good advisors. Talk to professionals, talk to your family, talk to friends, read books, periodicals and online sources. Borrow the brains of people smarter and more well-informed than you are. Exercise humility and ask for input. Asking for advice is difficult for some. Learn to crave it. After some digging, I found this quote from English poet George Chapman (1559 – 1634). *"Advice is seldom welcome; and those who want it the most always like it the least."* It seems that taking advice is like eating liver. It's good for you but doesn't taste very good going down. Hey, I should copyright that. I think people often do not seek advice because they don't want to hear "no" or they don't want to hear that their idea might be flawed. Address flaws, don't ignore them. Also, not all advice is good advice, but always be on the lookout for nuggets of truth. Make sure you are getting input from multiple people or sources.

Note: It takes no talent to be a critic or a pessimist. There will be no shortage of people able and willing to dismiss business ideas as folly, voice their objections, or simply say "That will never work." I have never been impressed by those who can raise opposition or objections; it is the person offering solutions who impresses me and gets my attention. It will be wise to receive both positive and negative input when formulating your business concept, but such input must also be constructive and provide valuable solutions. When you receive input, ask the person to explain why they feel the way they do. Asking "Why?" can reveal the reasons behind their opinions and can produce amazing nuggets of knowledge. It can also expose reasons for unhealthy prejudice and bias.

Step 4 - Document your assumptions. Here is where you need to be very honest with yourself. Understand that assumptions are not facts! Assumptions are theories. Create a list of all of your assumptions, good and bad. Perform Step 2 on all of your assumptions. Fact find. Get answers. Seek the truth. When a group of people share the same assumption(s), they falsely take the assumptions as fact. Be careful of those who agree with you. Try to find those who don't. Have the courage to ask questions. Assumptions will become your worst nightmare if you get them wrong. Wrong assumptions can lead to catastrophic results. I don't have an ancient proverb here, but I do have a nice quote from famous American author and scholar, William Lyon Phelps (1865 – 1943). ***"In a start-up company, you basically throw out all assumptions every three weeks."*** Not only is this accurate, but it's funny.

Let me just say, I am not trying to be "preachy" here. I am simply sharing some time-tested and proven tools that I and others have used to create successful and desired results. This stuff works.

What business is right for you?

If you have come to the realization that you would like to become a business owner, the next questions is, **What product or service would you like to (or should you) provide?** It's time to ponder a list of questions to see what kind of business owner you might be. Your questions should consider the following: (Go to Appendices – Complete **Appendix B**)

1. What are you good (proficient) at?
2. Do you currently have a hobby you are passionate about?
3. What do you enjoy doing?
4. What inspires you?

5. Which occupation will hold your attention?
6. Which option provides the best income opportunity?
7. Which option provides longevity?
8. What are the physical demands (wear and tear on your body)?
9. Would you rather use your mind or your back to get your job done?
10. Are you able to handle and enjoy repetition?
11. Are you able to handle rejection and negative criticism?
12. Which option is best for your family?
13. Which option provides the most flexibility?
14. Which option has the smallest barrier to entry?
15. What do the start-up costs look like for each option?
16. What are the education, certification, licensing, and credential requirements?
17. Which option will rejuvenate you?
18. Which option will deplete you?
19. Do you prefer to work with others or work alone?
20. Would you like to hire a staff to help run things or operate by yourself?
21. Would you rather speak or listen?
22. Would you prefer a retail store front or a retail website?
23. Would you rather market yourself by word of mouth or by running an ad?
24. Would you like to have your name on a store front or remain anonymous?

25. Do you prefer to have a large client list or relatively small one?
26. Do you desire to have passive income down the road?
27. Do you intend to sell your business one day?
28. Do you plan to hand your business down to someone else?
29. Which option will be impacted by business cycles or seasonal weather?
30. Do you prefer moderate steady income or larger income with volatility?
31. Do you prefer to work indoors or out?
32. Do you prefer physical labor and activity or prefer working from an office chair?
33. Do you prefer to travel, work on the road, or stay put?
34. Will your business be able to relocate if you decide to move?
35. Would you prefer to help existing clients or find new ones?
36. Do you prefer an existing business or would like to create a new company from scratch?
37. Would you rather talk to someone about something or actually do something?
38. Do you prefer a home-based office, commercial space, or store front?
39. Do you like to have structure or figure things out as you go?
40. Do you enjoy negotiations or do you prefer to have things fixed?
41. Would you rather see your clients happy or see a good income?
42. Would you rather invest money or time into your new business?
43. Do you prefer to be creative or administrative?

44. Would you rather work with machines or people?

45. How do you feel about adopting technology?

46. How do you feel about paperwork, reports, organization, and storage?

47. Would you prefer to explain your business to a person or group of people?

If you and I were in a meeting, these are the types of questions I would be asking you. As you filter through these questions, more than likely, you will come up with more questions on your own. Keep these questions and your answers in a spreadsheet or Word doc so you can refer to them and amend them as you progress. It will be normal for your predisposition toward certain business to evolve and change. The results might surprise you. They did for me, that's for sure.

When the idea of being an accountant was first introduced to me, my initial reaction was not very positive. I felt myself dismissing the suggestion. The CPA who suggested it gave me a few reasons why I should consider it. That was enough for me to take the suggestion seriously and see how being an accountant stacked up with the questions I have listed above. Using and answering these questions helped me to keep emotion, bias, and ignorance from having an impact on my decision. After subjecting the Accounting profession to the barrage of questions, Accountancy came out the other end looking like pure genius. I wish I could take credit for the idea, but as you now know, the idea wasn't mine.

Now, having subjected yourself to the list of questions, where do you go from here? Have you already narrowed down your list of possible businesses? Or are you confused as to which business you should pursue? Many readers of this book won't have their specific business ideas nailed down until after reading the entire book. Specifically, Chapters 3, 4, 6, and 8 could help narrow down your potential choices. It might even take a second reading of the book to help you make your decision. But sometimes the answer is right under your nose, or in your basement. It's your hobby.

Did you read question #2 above? It is quite common for my clients to create their new businesses from their hobbies. You will notice that your hobby or hobbies score well when subjected to the questions above. Growing a hobby into a business works well for many people. The ramp-up can be shorter, the learning curve reduced, the tools of the trade are most often present, the skill set is there, and the proficiency is there. Many of the necessary pieces are already in place. The hobby just needs some high-octane fuel and a good driver behind the wheel. Now, if you don't have a hobby you are passionate about, don't worry. I have another idea to help you. Grab a snack and head back to your computer.

Hey, did you read your StrengthsFinder 2.0 yet? Make sure you do that. It will help. However, if you still have no idea what kind of business you would like to start or what aptitudes you possess, you can try completing some assessments, templates, and self-tests. You can conduct online searches for **"small business readiness assessment," "new business planner templates," "self-assessment test," "career tests," "personality tests,"** and **"business owner self-assessment."** Taking the online tests should keep you busy for a while. If you need to take a break from the book to conduct your research, so be it. The book will understand. After you have gained some insight and conviction as to the direction you intend to take, you can return to the book and use it to hone your choices. I have designed this book to be patient. If it needs to allow you some time to think, it will. No worries here.

What does your business look like in your head and on paper?

If you are still reading this book, good for you. You might have what it takes to be a successful business owner. I was blunt in the first chapter to help sober you up if were too much of a Walter Mitty (fun movie if you haven't seen it yet). If your friends call you "DreamWeaver" or "DreamMachine," that might not be a good sign. It's good to be a visionary, but not so sure if it's good to be a dreamer. I worked in Hollywood for 10 years. The streets and restaurants are littered with dreamers who had visions of making it big as an actor, writer, director, or fashion model. Visionaries tend to be successful while dreamers tend to burn out. I want to encourage you to stop thinking about the allure or "concept" of being a business owner and start focusing on the reality of what your business really looks like on paper. Will it pencil out?

This is where old-fashioned research comes in to play. Your marketing plan will involve extensive research, so you might as well get started on it now. You will want to ponder questions such as:

- Can I really run a business?
- Where do I want to be in 5, 10, 15, and 20 years from now?
- What are the physical requirements?
- What is my income potential?
- Is the market saturated with my line of work?
- What are the trends for this type of business?
- Is my business dependent on the discretionary spending of my clients?
- What credentials, education, certifications, and continuing education are required?

- Will I have a home office or retail space?
- Will I be serviced-based or will I have inventory and sales tax to process?
- What is the potential for expansion?
- Is my industry recession proof?
- Can I relocate my business someday?
- Will it be personality or brand driven?
- Can I sell my business in the future?
- Does it have the potential to provide passive income?
- What furniture and tools are required?
- What are the tax benefits?
- What is my exposure to liability and malpractice?
- Will I be required to travel?
- Will my business involve sales?
- What will be my fixed and variable costs each year?
- How competitive is my industry and how do I stack up to my competitors?
- Do the benefits outweigh the costs? If so, by how much?
- What is my ramp-up period?
- How long before I am profitable?
- Will I enjoy my business in years to come or will the novelty wear off?
- Can I lose my job or be fired from my current company?

This list is in no way comprehensive. As you answer these questions, you will formulate more on your own. I suggest you write them down as they come to you and document your answers. You will want to refer to these questions and answers as time moves on to reevaluate your frame of mind.

Where do you see yourself in the near and distant future?

We touched on this question above with the 5, 10, 15, and 20-year outlook. I isolated it here because it is very important. Again, there is no right or wrong answer, but being realistic is essential. I know people who are thrilled with the concept of building a business, reaching a benchmark, then selling or dissolving the company. I am one of them. There is no problem with this strategy as long as that is the plan from day one. Some people get bored with the actual work but love the creation. Others love the creation AND love the work. Others don't like the creation but love the work. Of all the businesses I have started, BlackBull, by far, is the one I enjoy the most. I love building it (always a work in progress) and love working with my clients. I see myself running BlackBull well into my late 70's. BlackBull for me is the ultimate sweet spot as far as business ownership is concerned. However, when I started my tile contracting business at age 19, I knew I only wanted to set tile for four or five years until I was done with school and my knees and back were shot. I had a short-term plan going in.

Make sure you visualize yourself and where you will be in five-year increments. What will your health be like? What will your family be like as kids grow up and move out? Where will you be living? Again, you can refer to the list of questions above but please don't let time sneak up on you. You should have a plan in place way before the decades begin to roll past you.

Caution: Building a company can take its toll. You may not feel it much the first or second time around, but starting companies may eventually wear you out. Have you ever been fired or switched jobs? Remember what that first day felt like at your new company? Feeling lost, disconnected, and behind the curve is common. You know you need to ramp-up, gain speed and momentum, assimilate, and then be a valuable contributing member of your team or workplace. That ramp-up gets exhausting. Well, it does for me anyway. So, plan wisely. You will want to reduce the number of ramp-ups in your life. I believe professionals and business owners only have so many ramp-ups in them until they burn out, loose their spark, and become discouraged.

What services will you offer, how, and why?

For me, this is the part of the process where things start to get exciting. This question allows the vision to start taking shape. To address this, I flip the dynamic around. Rather than taking an egocentric position of being the greatest <u>(your trade)</u>, I ask myself, "Why on earth would anyone want to do business with me?" "What can I do or offer that isn't already being done?" "How will my business be better than the _____ business down the street?"

I am a student and admirer of business. I am still amazed that Starbucks can take a cup of coffee, charge $6 for it, and have a customer walk away happy like they were just handed a stack of pizzas. After all, we have been drinking coffee in America for over 200 years. Coffee is nothing new, folks. After the Boston Tea Party of 1773, large numbers of Americans switched to drinking coffee because drinking tea had become unpatriotic. Yet Starbucks has managed to make coffee drinking seem new and exciting.

So what is so special about Starbucks? Well, believe it or not, it's not about the coffee; it's about the experience. Starbucks isn't just selling coffee.

With each cup, they are delivering flavor, satisfaction, consistency, convenience, and status. People don't mind being seen holding a cup with a green logo on it. Some even flaunt the logo. It holds status. If it were just about a wonderful cup of coffee, lines would be out the door at 7-Eleven and AM/PM Mini Marts. Starbucks, Pete's, Seattle's Best, The Pannikin, and The Coffee Bean and Tea Leaf have all managed to repackage a centuries-old product. That, my friend, is sheer brilliance. Can you do the same?

How will you create a product or service that will make you stand out? When you think you have answered that question, you will want to test that theory out with a focus group of your peers. Create a survey and hand it out or send it out over social media. Run the idea past as many people as you can without jeopardizing your concept or product. There are some great survey templates at www.surveymonkey.com.

I have included a basic survey here:
(Go to Appendices - see **Appendix C**)

1. **What do you like most about our new product (service)?**

2. **What changes would most improve our new product (service)?**

3. **What do you like most about competing products (services) currently available from other companies?**

4. **What changes would most improve competing products (services) currently available from other companies?**

5. **What would make you more likely to use our new product (service)?**

6. **If our new product (service) were available today, how likely would you be to recommend it to others?**
    - ☐ Extremely likely
    - ☐ Very likely
    - ☐ Moderately likely
    - ☐ Slightly likely
    - ☐ Not likely at all

7. **If you are not likely to use our new product (service), why not?**
    - ☐ Do not need a product (service) like this
    - ☐ Do not want a product (service) like this
    - ☐ Satisfied with competing products (services) currently available
    - ☐ Cannot pay for a product (service) like this
    - ☐ Not willing to pay for a product (service) like this
    - ☐ Other (please specify):

8. **How important is price to you when choosing this type of company?**
    - ☐ Extremely important
    - ☐ Quite important
    - ☐ Moderately important
    - ☐ Slightly important
    - ☐ Not at all important

9. **Overall, how satisfied are you with your experience using our new product (service)?**
    - ☐ Extremely satisfied
    - ☐ Quite satisfied
    - ☐ Somewhat satisfied
    - ☐ Neither satisfied nor dissatisfied
    - ☐ Somewhat dissatisfied
    - ☐ Quite dissatisfied

☐ Extremely dissatisfied

10. **If our new product (service) were available today, how likely would you be to use it instead of competing products currently available from other companies?**
    ☐ Extremely likely
    ☐ Very likely
    ☐ Moderately likely
    ☐ Slightly likely
    ☐ Not likely at all

11. **If our new company were available today, how likely would you be to recommend it to others?**
    ☐ Extremely likely
    ☐ Very likely
    ☐ Moderately likely
    ☐ Slightly likely
    ☐ Not likely at all

12. **How important is convenience when choosing this type of product (service)?**
    ☐ Extremely important
    ☐ Quite important
    ☐ Moderately important
    ☐ Slightly important
    ☐ Not at all important

Are you starting from scratch or taking over an existing business?

Both of these options have merits. There is no right or wrong answer here. It really depends on your capabilities, comfort level, short-term and long-term needs, available assets, and the opportunities before you. I have created a side-by-side comparison graph for you to reveal some of the pros and cons. You can see they have an inverse relationship.

	Starting From Scratch		Purchase Existing Business	
	Pro	Con	Pro	Con
Cost	X			X
Level of risk *	X	X	X	X
Time to ramp-up		X	X	
Allows for learning curve	X			X
Easy to modify business plan	X			X
Build client base and income quickly		X	X	
Time to establish brand		X	X	
Maintaining client loyalty	X			X
Deciding location of company	X			X
Deciding brand and logo of company	X			X

* (It depends on specific issue)

Are you looking for the best of both worlds? This scenario too is possible. Many new business owners will purchase an existing business with an exit strategy. For instance, one of my clients recently took over a yoga studio assuming the client base, the name, the location, and everything else that came with it. Her intention was to slowly introduce her brand of service to her customer base then slowly transition the studio into the model she wants as if she was starting from scratch. The story of boiling a frog is a good analogy. Tossing a frog into hot water will cause it to jump out (clients leave), but if the water temperature slowly rises, the frog doesn't notice the change and slowly cooks into a delicious treat (clients stay). Is that a gross analogy?

Sorry.

Fact: Many, if not most, business owners are very poor business people. Have you read ***The E-Myth (Revisited)***? If not, you might want to do so. You can purchase it for under $12 on Amazon.com.

*"In this first new and totally revised edition of the 150,000-copy underground bestseller, The E-Myth, Michael Gerber dispels the myths surrounding starting your own business and shows how commonplace **assumptions** can get in the way of running a business. He walks you through the steps in the life of a business from entrepreneurial infancy, through adolescent growing pains, to the mature entrepreneurial perspective, the guiding light of all businesses that succeed. He then shows how to apply the lessons of franchising to any business whether or not it is a franchise. Finally, Gerber draws the vital, often overlooked distinction between working on your business and working in your business. After you have read The E-Myth Revisited, you will truly be able to grow your business in a predictable and productive way."* (www.amazon.com)

The premise here is that "Technicians" should not necessarily be managers, supervisors, or business owners. There is a big difference between a good worker and a good businessperson. Just because an electrician is good at running wire, does not mean he or she will be good at running a company or managing the books, the clients, and the staff. There is no shortage of businesses for sale or owners who want to get out because they bit off more than they could chew. The E-Myth concept creates great opportunities for true business people who are looking for ripe opportunities to grab a business for pennies-on-the-dollar. It is encouraging knowing there are amazing opportunities out there, but discouraging to see the true amount of talent, skill, and effort it takes to make a business successful.

Caution: When you see an apparently "successful" or "failing" business, pause before you start making judgments. Your eyes could be deceiving you. I know business owners who speak broken English, have little to no people skills, and are running dirty and out-of-date businesses in bad parts of town, but are pulling net incomes in the hundreds of thousands of dollars. It's mind blowing. At the same time, I have seen extremely impressive businesses and store fronts shut down without notice time after time. It only takes a walk to the local neighborhood shopping strip to see the astronomical failure rate of seemingly "successful" businesses. Fancy signs and corner locations don't ensure much of anything. Successful businesses are not one-dimensional but require quality and efficiency at all levels if longevity is the goal.

Chapter 3

The Business Plan

What is a business plan and do you need one?

Um, yeah, you should have one. Even if you only create an executive summary, a business plan puts all thoughts on paper. The business plan creates a blueprint of your business concept so it can be analyzed by you and other stakeholders. A business plan is a mechanism or tool which asks all the questions that need to be answered when constructing a business. It reveals strengths and weaknesses. Since informal business plans are directed mainly at the new owner, some feel it is not essential. Formal business plans are essential if a new business owner intends to secure small business loans or attract venture capital (VC). Very few business owners I have dealt with have ever required VC. SBA and personal loans usually do the trick. I personally have only required VC for one of my business ventures. The business plan I wrote was 347 pages, yet the executive summary was only 45. The business included manufacturing for a global market. Most local, small businesses could probably benefit from a 10 – 20 page executive summary and be just fine. Here are 10 benefits business owners receive when utilizing a business plan:

1. **You will stay on target** - It's hard to stick to a strategy through the daily routine and interruptions. A business plan summarizes the main points of your strategy and is a reminder of what it includes and rules out.

2. **Business objectives will be clear** - Use your plan to define and manage

specific measurable objectives like web visitors, sales, margins or new product launches. Define success in objective terms.

3. **Your educated guesses will be better** - Use your plan to refine your educated guesses about things like potential market, sales, costs of sales, sales drivers, lead processing and business processes.

4. **Priorities will make more sense** - Aside from the strategy, there are also priorities for other factors of your business like growth, management and financial health. Use your plan to set a foundation for these. Revise as the business evolves.

5. **You will understand interdependencies** - Use a plan to keep track of what needs to happen and in what order. For example, if you need to coordinate a product release with a testing schedule, or a marketing plan with a product release, your business plan can be invaluable in keeping you organized and on track.

6. **Milestones will keep you on track** - Use a business plan to keep track of dates and deadlines in one place. This is valuable even for the one-person business and vital for teams.

7. **You will be better at delegating** - The business plan is an ideal place to clarify who is responsible for what job or task. Every important task should have one person in charge. Your plan keeps track.

8. **Managing team members and tracking results will be easy** - So many people acknowledge the need for regular team member reviews and just as many admit that they hate the reviews. The plan is a great format for getting things in writing and following up on the differences between expectations and results with course corrections.

9. **You can better plan and manage cash flow** - No business can afford to mismanage cash. Simple profits are rarely the same as cash. A cash flow plan is a great way to tie together educated guesses on sales, costs, expenses, assets you need to buy, and debts you have to pay.

10. **Course corrections will keep your business from flopping** - Having a business plan gives you a way to be proactive, not reactive, about business. Don't wait for things to happen. Plan for them. Follow up by tracking the results and making course corrections. It's a myth that a business plan is supposed to predict the future. Instead it sets goals, states assumptions, and drafts a course of action.

Where can you get help?

Finding a business plan outline is not difficult. You can do an online search for "Business Plan Template" and find 25,600,000 results in .26 seconds. Not too shabby. You can also use the Small Business Development Center (SBDC) or Service Corps of Retired Executives (SCORE) for help. I have added two very basic business plan outlines for you. (Go to Appendices – see **Appendix D**)

Warning: When you first look at the business plan templates online, it can be overwhelming and make you want to go play with your dog instead. Remember, you are looking at formal templates. If you focus on the section headings, you will see the value of the business plan emerge. Don't be distracted by the overwhelming details. Focus on the main content. You will see that the business plan is addressing the same questions you have floating in your head already.

The main topics to consider

I want to encourage you to relax and take the business plan in stride. Under each section, you will want to focus on the sub-sections that apply to your business. When your business first starts out, it might be relatively basic. This is normal. As your business grows, you might find you begin to incorporate more of the sub-sections in your business plan.

For instance, a small business owner I know started cooking and baking gluten-free foods. She would just rent a commercial kitchen and had no storefront or kitchen of her own. At that point, her business model and plan was quite simple. Purchase ingredients, rent a kitchen for four hours, and sell what she baked to her friends. As demand grew, so did her needs. She eventually expanded into a restaurant of her own and is doing quite well. She has already outgrown her current location and is looking to move again. And what happens if she starts to ship her products or get into frozen food distribution? Well, more sub-sections of her business plan will need to be addressed. It's ok to take it as it comes. Rome wasn't built in a day. To be practical, here are the main sections and sub-sections you will want to consider:

Executive Summary
The executive summary is my favorite part. It addresses all the basic questions you or a partner should have without going into mind-numbing detail. The length of the executive summary is usually in direct correlation with the length of time you have had your business. For start-ups, there is not as much "nut-n-bolt" information to share. Make up for that by explaining the experience you bring, your background, and your special skill sets. Here are some of the areas you will want to address in the executive summary:

- **The Mission Statement** (Venture Description):
Explain what your business is all about. Why is it exciting and relevant? What is your business philosophy? How do you want to impact others, the environment, your community, your churches, your schools, your family, etc.? This is the place to really show others who you are and why you are different. This is where your passion shines. It can reveal why you wanted to start a business in the first place.

- **Company Information:**
Name the founders of your company, when it was formed, the number of employees, and your location. Explain how the company and staff will be structured and managed.

- **Services Provided:**
Briefly explain and describe the services you provide.

- **Marketing and Growth Highlights:**
Summarize your company's growth including client base, revenues, and market share. State the benchmarks you have reached.

- **Financial Information:**
State your current financial position, current financial needs, and future needs. List any investors or stakeholders you have.

- **Future Goals:**
Explain where you would like to take your business and what your plans for growth look like.

Management

In the management section, you will want to explain or outline the inner workings of your business. You will want to address the following areas:

•Form of Business Entity:

Most small businesses get off the ground operating as a Sole Proprietorship. This takes very little legal action to establish (or no action at all in some cases) and has a business owner up and running in no time. You just decide, "I want to start a tree trimming business." So, you knock on the neighbor's door, ask to trim their tree, they say yes, you trim the tree, collect $50 from your neighbor and, BAM!, you are a business owner, baby! It's really that easy. You will eventually file a Schedule-C on your personal tax return (for your business) which attaches to your 1040. The crazy thing is many, if not most, business owners will keep this form of legal entity and never graduate to the next level. Becoming an LLC or S-Corporation can provide more security and benefits for the business owner as the business grows. Most likely, creating a C-Corporation will not be in your future unless you eclipse 100 shareholders. When that day comes, you will need much more than this handy book.

Here is a word you need to know and understand: **liability**. As a business owner, you will need to perpetually limit and reduce your exposure to liability. Liability is a ticking time bomb that can take a company down immediately or over time. You will want to stay away from malpractice, misrepresentation, injury, fraud, discrimination, harassment, and the like. Having an LLC (Limited Liability Company) or an S-Corporation provides a degree of separation between owner and business. I could write a 300-page book just outlining LLC's and S-Corp's. I am not going to do that here, but I can provide the aerial view.

When you maintain your business as an LLC or S-Corporation, you are an employee of your company. You own it on paper, but your company has its own identity. If someone wants to sue you, they will discover you are simply an employee. They will need to sue your company. The liability will transfer to your company and keep your personal life and finances out of the line of fire. Remember our tree trimmer? As a sole proprietor, what happens if his or her truck runs over the leg of the neighbor's son? His or her entire business and personal life can come crashing down. But what happens if the truck is in the name of the company and our tree trimmer is simply an employee of the company? The liability is carried by the company, not our tree trimmer. The company's entity structure should keep the tree trimmer's family and home safe and sound.

Disclaimer: An insurance policy and/or a bond should always be present regardless of the business entity. Again, I am being extremely simplistic here to try and make a point. You will need to invest in a deeper understanding to properly implement an LLC or S-Corp. As a general business rule, I don't try to convince my clients to do anything. Each client has their own comfort level. I feel it is my job to offer suggestions to my clients and help educate them. This is all I am doing here. Decisions made are ultimately up to the client. As a general rule, you will want to make sure you and your company are licensed, bonded, and insured to cover the bases.

•**Decision Makers:**
This is not a difficult area to address. A sole proprietorship usually has only one decision maker, themselves; hence the word "sole." There might be others who have some control over bank accounts or are potential decision makers in the event of injury, illness, or death. A Power of Attorney (POA) could be drafted to help with this. A POA can allow a surrogate decision maker to make decisions when the primary decision maker is unavailable or incapacitated. When other decision makers and partners are added to your team, you may want to document them and their responsibilities. You might

provide a small resume or biography on each member. A LinkedIn-style profile also works well.

•Sphere of Influence (Advisors) and Infrastructure:
Starting out, the only advisor on your team might be yourself. Here, you can also add those "non-partners" who are contributing to your company in an advisory role. If you have your go-to advisors addressing your needs when it comes to banking, marketing, insurance, legal issues, management, and advertising, you might want to list them in this section.

•Employee Hiring Protocol:
This is a great time to explain an "If / Then" protocol when it comes to hiring. "If" we need to expand and hire "Then" the company will do the following... Some business owners like to hire and promote from within. If you decide to hire, understand the employee's rights. Others will avoid all the payroll tax issues and use temp agencies to scout and pre-screen their employees. Using a temp agency provides amazing flexibility and the ability to hire a very specific employee for each task. You can visit www.bestofstaffing.com to view the nation's best staffing companies. To find the staffing companies in your area, perform an internet search with "(your city) staffing agencies."
Internal hires and temp agencies both have pros and cons to consider. Using sub-contractors is also a viable option.

Using sub-contractors will require the issuance of Form 1099-Misc at year-end and will not require the impounding and payment of payroll taxes. Caution: The IRS has very specific guidelines about the "employee" vs. "independent contractor" designation. All too often, business owners elect to call their employees independent contractors to avoid carrying worker's compensation insurance and dealing with the payroll tax issues. Do Not fall into this common trap. Please refer to the IRS webpage titled "Small Businesses & Self-Employed: Independent Contractor, Self-Employed or

Employee" and review IRS Form SS-8 before making any decisions.

•Communications:

The communication policy you decide upon is an extremely important piece of your company's business model. Every communication made between employees, clients, and stakeholders conveys a message, leaves a trail, and can affect the company's brand, both in positive and negative ways. Written communications (letters, texts, and emails) are the ones with which you should be most careful. It is very easy for a person to misunderstand or misinterpret the written word. In addition, words leave a permanent record. This can be favorable or damaging depending on the nature of the content communicated. The rule of thumb here – use written words to convey very simplistic concepts. If a communication is wordy, detailed, or requires more than a few lines, pick up the phone! Don't be lazy. Over the years, I have seen emails and texts backfire and leave trails of damage and destruction. Please don't learn the hard way.

You will want to establish a strict communication policy of do's and don'ts. This will be included in your employment contracts. The communication policy can include permitted and/or banned activities, pre-written templates, and manager approvals. For my businesses, the communication policy was always at the top of the list. Employees generally will not understand the critical nature of communications and may even find the strict policies to be silly. Don't forget, employees either help or hurt your brand. Perhaps you will need to educate them about potential liability for them to grasp the seriousness of the issue. I would stress that violations of the communication policy could lead to immediate termination. If this sounds insensitive or extreme to a business owner, I highly recommend learning more about liability and misrepresentation and how it can negatively impact a business.

Improper communications can lead to:

- Termination
- Public embarrassment
- Information leaks
- Trade secret leaks
- Spam
- Legal issues
- Database corruption
- Clogging exchange queues
- Communication overload
- Criminal charges
- Communication failure
- Viruses
- Regulation violations
- Network failures
- Power outages
- Being blacklisted

•Compensation Structure:
Stakeholders will need to understand the company's ownership structure and control of shares (does not include sole proprietors). It is not uncommon to outline how revenues will be used to cover company expenses and operational costs before owner's draws are executed. Don't forget, most new companies will lose money before they break even and produce a cash flow. At year-end, we can reconcile your draws and contributions to determine your owner's equity. We can also do a year-end payroll and issue your W-2 wages if desired. If you are going to collect W-2 wages as an employee of your company, you do not need to report wages every two weeks. Year-end payroll processing works just fine.

For a new business owner, operating a business at a loss can seem discouraging at face value; however, this is a normal part of the business life cycle. If the business is profitable after year one, consider yourself to be quite fortunate. If and when a business does lose money, that loss translates into a very attractive tax deduction and can be worth quite a bit of money at tax time. You will want to take measures to minimize your losses, but do not be afraid of them.

Services provided

It's great to finally talk about services! This is always exciting. This helps reveal why you wanted to start a business in the first place. It exposes your passions, the problems in the marketplace, and the solutions you offer. A client or customer learns more about the business owner and the company simply by understanding the services provided. Your website will be a great tool for you to help convey your story, philosophy, and services. We will get into the marketing piece a little further on. For now, let's look at some of the basics you should be addressing when talking about your services. As you probably know, services or products provided don't really mean much of anything until your consumer understands the features and benefits you are providing.

•**Features & Benefits:**
At the risk of insulting your intelligence, let's review features and benefits. The Feature- A customer needs to know "What" you are offering. A clear description of the product or service is essential. The Benefit- A customer needs to know "Why or How" it will benefit or help them. The feature attracts attention, the benefit builds the value. If this relationship is still confusing for you, go to Amazon.com and look at product for sale. You will see the features and benefits outlined in the product description- physical properties, what it does, how it works, and reviews. But at this point, I will assume you are up to speed, so let's move on.

•**Service Directive:**
The service directive can be your Mission Statement or part of your mission statement. It tells the public what you think, why your company is amazing, and how you intend to make the world a better place. In so many words, it lets others know why you started your business in the first place. The service directive can be a secret you keep to yourself or the branded cornerstone

you build your business upon. When a client or customer asks themselves, "Why would I want to do business with (your company)?", the answer provides the rationale convincing them to support your company.

- **Service Limitations and Liability:**

Most business owners only think about all the amazing services or products they are going to offer. They rarely think about what they DON'T want to offer. It is perfectly fine not being the Jack-of-All-Trades and limiting what your company does. In fact, many companies are successful because they don't offer everything. Have you ever heard of Costco? Costco is the nation's second largest retailer because they have adopted this model. It will be important for you to think about this. There are things you won't want to do or offer for a few reasons:

- You simply don't like to offer the product or perform the service
- The product or service:
    - is dangerous
    - is depleting
    - is not profitable
    - is too specialized
    - is too labor intensive
    - opens the door to government regulation
    - undermines your specialization
    - requires certifications you don't possess
    - requires tools and facilities you don't have
    - creates a liability
    - requires insurance you don't have
    - would force you to hire help
    - would reduce the quality of your other services
    - would require you to travel
    - would extend your work day or work week

•Government Oversight:

Here we take a closer look at bullet point #5 above (government regulation). Depending on the number and type of services or products you intend to offer, federal, state, or municipal government entities could be involved. I do not recommend you shy away from any services requiring government permits, certificates, or approval. I am simply saying that you need to take them seriously and prepare in advance for such regulations. You would not want to provide non-compliant services only to be fined or shutdown at a later time. This is a pitfall you will most definitely want to avoid. Remember, ***"An ounce of prevention is worth a pound of cure."*** Make sure any necessary permits, licenses, or certificates are built into your new business start-up process.

•Facility and Operations:

Your short-term goals may differ from your long-term goals, and they probably should. Perhaps in the short-term, you will want to start small when considering your facility and operations. Of course, you don't have to. It's just a common and often wise position to take. You can start small by opening a home office or by taking over an existing business and its location. You do not need to re-invent the wheel here. After your business gains traction and revenues grow, you might have the capital to make a big move into another space or even open multiple locations. This also holds true for your operations. Do you watch Cake Boss? Buddy's bakery empire is rising faster than his bread dough.

You can keep your operations bridled until revenues and demands are pushing you from behind. In fact, it is very common for a small business owner to expand reluctantly because they are forced into it. Remember my restaurant owner friend? That is what happened to her.

- **Ancillary Products or Services:**

As your business grows, do you intend to add the products or services you initially were not capable of offering or simply chose not to offer? As client demands grow, you may be forced to expand your services or product line to stay current and competitive. In addition, I am well aware of business owners who offer a service they absolutely do not want to offer simply to give the impression that they are full-service.

For instance, a yard maintenance company might offer tree trimming as part of its list of services. The reality is, the owner might be terrified of heights and would never dream of trimming trees. However, since most reputable yard care companies offer tree trimming, this owner also offers the service. They, of course, will not trim the trees themselves. They will contract the work out, have a fearless employee handle it, or simply bid the job so high that the customer goes with another company. The point here, counter to their convictions, the business owner still offered a service they do not feel good about. The overall image of being a full-service provider is good for the company brand and goodwill. That takes precedence over the company owner's personal bias.

Now, let's flip this hypothetical situation. It is also possible for a company to retract services and products offered to remain profitable and specialized. Let's take a look at In-N-Out Burger. Why is their business model so insanely successful? In-N-Out Burger offers very few menu items but executes them perfectly. Too many selections and choices can confuse and frustrate customers. In-N-Out customers, even those visiting In-N-Out for the first time, master the menu in the few seconds or minutes they wait in line. Contrast that with the overwhelming breakfast or regular menus from McDonalds and Jack-In-The-Box and you can see why In-N-Out is the restaurant of choice for millions of Americans. There is a learning curve necessary with restaurants offering an abundance of choices. Ordering takes time to filter the menu. To some extent, an abundance of choices has some appeal, but there is a point at which it begins to have a negative and opposite effect. It is common, and perhaps recommended, for a business owner to start initially with a long list of services or products. As popular and profitable services and products begin to reveal themselves, the business owner can redirect resources to mirror the demand. Less popular or less profitable products and services can be improved to reduce the trend, or can be phased out. Product or service phase-outs boost the company's specialization. This is a good thing.

Marketing

Lucky for me, I find marketing to be immensely fascinating. Before I secured a degree and a future in accounting, my background was in marketing. I am equally passionate about both marketing and accounting these days. As a boy, I grew up completely in love with fishing. I found it so amazing that a fish, a wild fish, would attack and try to eat the rubber, plastic, or wooden fishing lures I tossed out there and reeled in. The same epiphany hit me back in 2000 when I was involved in new product development and patents.

Have you heard of Pogs, the Pet Rock, the Rubik's Cube, and Beany Babies? They all seem like those fishing lures I used to toss around at my local lakes. People were buying up these products by the millions. It was all so unbelievable to me, so surreal. Why on earth would anyone with half a brain (fish) want to spend their hard earned money on a Pet Rock (lure)? This question caused me to fall head-over-heals in love with the science and phenomenon called marketing.

I would ask, "Are people foolish?", "Are they stupid?", "Or are they simply predictable based on a set of established human behavioral traits?" The answer was there all along behind curtain number three. The more I studied human behavior, the more I learned that human behavior and conditioning is not all that complicated. Of course, there are countless studies out there showing how colors, fonts, content, and messaging all play a critical role in consumer response to products, websites, brochures, PowerPoint presentations, and business cards. But there is something else the salt-of-the-earth, no-frills, businessperson has going for them. There is a tool unmatched by any clever company name or fancy four-color brochure. It's called **value.**

Ralph Waldo Emerson famously said "If a man has good corn or wood, or boards, or pigs, to sell, or can make better chairs or knives, crucibles or church organs, than anybody else, you will find a broad hard-beaten road to his house, though it be in the woods." This has been misquoted over time into the better-known quote, ***"Build a better mousetrap, and the world will beat a path to your door."*** But do you understand the point here? Provide a great product or service at a great price and the people and money will follow. Clever company names, fancy signage, flashy brochures, they are great, but they are not products. They won't mean a hill of beans if your products and services are not quality and priced fairly. Don't lose sight of what matters most.

•Industry Analysis:
As a business owner, one of the first things you need to do is analyze the industry you are entering. You should already be curious about many things and have lists of questions that need answers. To help you along, I have provided some of the questions you might want to consider.

- What barriers to entry does this industry have?
- What does the competition look like (direct and indirect)?
- What about the potential for future competition?
- What are the price points?
- Is the industry growing, contracting, or insulated and stable?
- Does the industry have growth potential or is the market already saturated?
- What trends do you see?
- How is technology impacting this industry?
- Is the industry seasonal?
- What are your company's strengths and weaknesses?
- What are your company's advantages and disadvantages?

This list is not comprehensive or set in stone. You may add to it as you wish. You will be able to address many, if not most, of your questions with online research and trips to the local library. Online Yellow Page listings, as well as search engine results can keep you busy for days or weeks compiling all of your data. You can also consider performing a SWOT analysis (Strengths, Weaknesses, Opportunities, and Threats). Keep your data well organized in Excel Spreadsheets for later access and analysis. (Go to Appendices – see **Appendix E** for SWOT Analysis example)

•**Local Market Profile:**
The industry analysis was broad-brush. Now you need to take a look at your specific market in more detail. It will be important for you to understand the competition, trends, and activities in your local market. "Local" could mean different things to different business owners. A local carwash could be the

corner car wash servicing the local neighborhoods. A local hospital could be servicing 500,000 residents in a 10-mile radius. You will want to determine your target market in your local market.

If you own a yoga studio, your target market is not going to be anyone who can fog a mirror. Your target market will be a very specific type of person. It will be wise for you to collect the demographics for your local neighborhood. You can try visiting www.city-data.com, enter your desired zip codes, and mine the data. Pull what you need and add to your spreadsheets. Www.zip-codes.com also provides some good data that might be worth exploring. When targeting a specific type of person, you can visit the website www.referenceusa.com (it requires your library card to access it). The internet is amazing and provides mind-saturating data with a just a few clicks of a mouse, but don't forget to physically canvass your neighborhoods as well.

Take a walk, ride a bike, drive around with the top down, as long as you are physically pouring over your potential markets, you are doing yourself and your company a big favor. You will be amazed at what you learn. Be analytical when you are on your field trip. Learn to ask WHY. Ask yourself:

- Why is that business so appealing to me?
- Why does this strip mall always look so dead?
- Why is the vacancy rate so high around here?
- Why does this strip mall seem to have no turn over?
- Why is there no parking?
- Why were all the trees cut down?
- Why is there an armed guard in front of that bank?
- Why is there no graffiti on that block wall?

- Why would my clients want to come here?
- Why is this rent so cheap (or expensive)?
- Why does that car look abandoned? ...And on and on.

With smart phones, you may not need to take anything else with you. Your phone will have your maps, camera, note pad, and voice recorder. If you don't have a smart phone, grab your iPad or take a camera and a notepad to document your trips. In addition, I would canvass your neighborhoods during the week and on weekends to observe the activity. You will also want to see what the neighborhoods look like during the day and at night. While on your joy ride, make sure you pop in to your competitors' businesses. You had better believe that the day you open your doors they will be visiting you. This is quite normal.

When first thinking about your direct and indirect competition, most business owners mistakenly assume that competition is bad. Not so. If this were the case, why are there often 2-3 gas stations at the same intersection? Why is Burger King across the street from McDonalds? Why is there a "Restaurant Row" in every community? Obviously, competition is not bad. If you know how to position yourself, you might actually prefer to have some local competition. This is the philosophy behind the auto dealership's "Mile of Cars" and medical plazas. You can even approach a business owner (outside of your market) with a similar business and ask to interview them. If you do, be prepared to have them ask you who you are and where you are from. Have an answer ready. You can have them field every question you will need answered for your business plan and cash flow projections. They do not have to know you are starting a similar business.

If you have a better product, better pricing, or better service, you can easily steal market share from a company who may have spent years doing much of the hard work for you. I encourage you to step back and look at things with the eyes of a savvy business person. You may need to change your perspective. It also might be wise to approach your competitors, announce you will be opening your business soon, and even see how you both might be able to collaborate to help each other. When it comes to the competitive analysis, I could easily draft another 100-page manuscript on the subject. We don't have room for that here. If you still have questions which need some input after you complete this book and your research, feel free to contact me.

•Price Point:
Are you still trying to figure out how to price your products or services? Well, get used to it. You might be working on that for a few years. As an accountant, I still tweak my pricing after every tax season. I never stop adjusting my pricing. Some pricing goes up, some comes down. Some services I decide to offer for free, and there are some formerly free services for which I now decide to charge. There is absolutely nothing wrong with keeping your pricing a work-in-progress.

When starting off, you might feel inclined to offer discount pricing. This is quite normal. If you intend to do this, it is better to discount your standard pricing for a period of time, than to start with a low price. Starting with a low standard price will force you to raise prices down the road. Raising prices too much can erode consumer confidence and backfire. The most important issue is to make sure the clients and customers always receive a sense of value when conducting business with your company. This is very important.

Have you considered the way in which you intend to charge your customers? Do fixed-rate services make sense? Should you be billing by the hour? What about a combination of the two? Both approaches have merit. If you really want to provide an amazing experience for customers, you might even let them choose in some cases. When you own your own small company, you can make up the rules as you go.

Let's say you own a bakery. You bake and decorate custom cakes for $50/hour. You know that all the custom cakes you make take no more than two hours each, but a new customer thinks $50 per hour is absurd. This customer's budget is $200, but she thinks it will take you at least six hours to create the cake she wants. At six hours, that's a $300 cake. If you offer to do it for $200, she will be very happy and you will earn $100 per hour instead of your standard $50 per hour. Both parties make out. Be careful, but don't be afraid to experiment with your pricing. Don't forget, if something doesn't go quite right, you can always make it up to the customer and still perpetuate and protect your brand value.

I believe it was Winston Churchill who famously said (in so many words), **"Pigs get fat, hogs get slaughtered."** When it comes to your pricing, you will want to heed these words. Pigs get fat by eating a little bit, but eating all the time. Doing this, they don't ever get big enough to start looking like a meal themselves. Hogs on the other hand, eat large amounts all day, every day. As a result, they start to look really yummy to farmers with shotguns. Do you see the parallel here? Price your goods or services at a fair level that keeps your lights on and feeds your family. This will ensure your business will be around for years to come. If you start to get greedy like a hog and continually raise your prices to try to afford a bigger house, car, or boat, your customers will eventually turn on you like the farmer with the gun. Your business can lose its goodwill, be on the road to obsolescence, and looking down the barrel of a hungry farmer's shotgun. Not good.

- **Branding:**

I love branding. Branding is one of the goals or byproducts of marketing. Some will confuse logos with brands. They are not the same. A logo can be the face of a brand, but a brand represents so much more than a logo.

The Starbucks logo conveys the message of, or reminds the consumer about, the Starbuck's brand. The brand includes the logo, but also includes the hospitality, the convenience, the consistency, the deliciousness, the aroma, the warmth, the refreshment, the friendliness, and the smiles associated with a visit to a Starbucks store. When a solid brand is established, the business owner is empowered. Brand loyalty allows a business owner to increase pricing (within reason), boost client retention, allow for expansion, experiment with new products and services, get away with mistakes from time to time, and increase new business.

You will never reach a day in which you say, "Whew! I finally got all of the company branding done." Companies never stop branding. Ford Motors has been around for over 100 years. Who on earth has not heard about Ford? No one within Ford's market target, I assure you, but Ford continues to market its brand each and every day. Every car that rolls off the assembly line either expands or damages the Ford brand depending on the owner's experience with his or her new car. Even when your company is up and running and doing well, you will still want to maintain a campaign to expand and reinforce your brand. When it comes to your company branding, you will want to ask yourself the following:

- Do I want a professional feel?
- Do I want to keep things casual?
- Will I have uniforms or a dress code?
- How will I communicate with clients and customers?
- What will my business cards look like?
- What will my logo look like?

- How will my website look and work?
- What will be my company colors?
- What is my client service policy?
- Will I be using social media?
- Will I have any print ads?
- Will I be offering coupons and discounts?
- What are my days and hours of availability?
- What is my return policy?
- Will I offer any guarantees?

Feel free to add to this list as you go. Each question is rather broad. Without too much effort, you can add 5-10 sub questions under each main question. For instance, if you answer "Yes" to question #3 (dress code) and want to have uniforms, now you need to ask yourself all the questions about color, design, hat, shoes, belts, ties, aprons, etc. Make sure you are using Word or Excel (or the like) so you can make changes easily. Paper and pen do not work here.

Finances

•Start-Up Costs:

Depending on the type of business you are starting, your start-up costs will vary greatly. A freelance writer needs very little to start a business; however, a full-service dentist will require tens of thousands of dollars of tools, equipment, and space. When you start to wrap your head around start-up costs, here are some areas you might want to consider: (the □ allows you to check them off as you acquire them) (Go to Appendices - see **Appendix H**)

- Office (professional office or home office)
    - [ ] Computer
    - [ ] Printer / Scanner
    - [ ] Flat screen monitors
    - [ ] Software
    - [ ] Desks
    - [ ] Credenza/hutch
    - [ ] File cabinets
    - [ ] Chairs
    - [ ] Tables
    - [ ] Plants
    - [ ] Lighting
    - [ ] Organizers
    - [ ] Whiteboard
    - [ ] Artwork
    - [ ] Coffee station
    - [ ] Mini Fridge
    - [ ] Office supplies
- Certifications
- Memberships and Subscriptions
- Legal Services
- Licenses
- Insurance
- Bond
- Printing
    - [ ] Business cards
    - [ ] Flyers
    - [ ] Tri-folds
    - [ ] POP displays

- ☐ Coupons
- ☐ Folders
- ☐ Letterhead
- Website
- Leases - space and equipment (and security deposits)

When starting a business from scratch, you will be wise to buddy up with **Craigslist, eBay, Amazon,** and **Overstock** (.com) to find the majority of your office hard goods for pennies on the dollar. As other business owners decide to downsize or close their doors, they will liquidate their hard goods. I have turned to Craigslist for many of my office furnishings. As your cash flow increases down the road, you can splurge for the office furniture set you really want. **Ikea** is also a great fishing hole for furnishings and furniture. As a bonus, www.ikea.com will now ship to your home. I have done very well over the years furnishing my office spaces with Ikea products. A fieldtrip to Ikea is well worth it. Oh, and don't forget thrift stores and garage sales. When purchasing second-hand goods, however, make sure they look nice. Appearance does matter.

It will be common for a client or customer to compliment the way your space looks if it truly looks nice, but you will rarely hear a customer tell you what they don't like about your space. That would be insulting. So, while you might feel your office looks great, your clients may not think so and you won't know the difference. This is why when starting out on a tight budget, select nice-looking furniture and furnishings and make sure you maintain them. Do not allow your office to become messy, disorganized, and dusty. I recommend that you or someone else take a step back and look at your office from a distance every few weeks. See what needs to be cleaned, repaired, touched up, or thrown away. And for goodness sake, take care of your plants. Vibrant plants can really make an office space look amazing. I recommend looking into a plant service; they are quite affordable.

When purchasing your items, make sure you do not pay top dollar for them. Try not to be cheap; the goal is to receive great value for your purchase. Spending $500 for a used desk might not seem cheap, but knowing that the desk originally sold for $1,500 makes that desk a great buy. In addition, when making your purchases, keep track of the item, price paid, and date of purchase on your spreadsheets. You will need this for your tax return and depreciation expenses.

- **Capital Requirements:**

Now that you have an idea of the items you will need to begin your business, you can put a budget together. It will be wise to estimate not only the immediate start-up costs, but also include the first year of operating costs. This will give you a realistic snapshot of where you are financially and create an expectation for revenues. Once your financial picture is clear, it might be time for some give-and-take.

Say for instance you are given $10 and are told that you can order anything you desire at McDonalds for lunch. After looking at the menu, there might be 50+ combinations of how you can spend that $10. You might find yourself in a scenario similar to this when comparing your start-up costs to your capital on hand. It might require some give-and-take. Perhaps the wall art purchase is delayed for a more critical item like your website development. Perhaps your custom folders can wait so that you can afford the software you need. Starting an office or business space is not an all-or-nothing proposition. You will start with the essentials and then mix in the ancillary items as time and money permit.

After your first-year budget is formulated, it's time to reconcile your assets on hand. You will need to figure out what office and business items you already have and deduct them from the budget. Then you calculate the balance needed to purchase the remaining items. Once you have that number, you need to see what cash assets you have on hand. If you have a cash surplus, you are good to go. If you have a cash deficit, you will need to eliminate items you intended to purchase, see what can be purchased on credit (if fiscally sound), discover other sources of capital, account for projected revenues, or a combination of all four.

- **Source of Capital:**

The first and most obvious question when starting out is, "Do you have the money?" Having the money up front is the best scenario to be in. Well, let me expand on that. Having the money up front, without the need of outside assistance, is the best scenario to be in. When the money to start your business is yours alone, it eliminates other decision makers. This gives you total control of your business. The ancient proverb reads, ***"Too many cooks spoil the broth."*** Sometimes in business, having too many decision makers is bad for the business and could cause the business to fail. On the other hand, without outside capital, some businesses would never get off the ground in the first place. If you are short on cash, you have a few options:

Look to friends and family to invest: As often is the case, your friends and family members might already be aware of your intentions to start a business. Those close to you might even be the ones pushing you to start a business. This close circle of people might already believe in your business concept and believe in you. They may even be offering unsolicited money to you to get you started. You will want to have serious conversations with these people. This could be the answer you have been looking for. They might require very little of you yet provide priceless support. **Caution:** <u>Mixing family and friends with business and money can get very dicey very quickly</u>. Forget the hugs and handshakes here. Ironclad agreements on paper are a must. Neither party should be relying on friendship or trust. It's all about the contracted agreement. The personal relationships are just a bonus. All expectations and concerns need to be addressed up front. Losing a family member or friend over money is NOT worth it.

Crowdfunding: With the passing of President Obama's JOBS Act this past April, the word of the day seems to be "crowdfunding." While this concept has arguably been around for centuries, it is still formally recognized as a new industry to many consumers, particularly those outside the United States. Crowdfunding is by definition, *"the practice of funding a project or venture by raising many small amounts of money from a large number of people, typically via the Internet"* (Forbes Magazine, 2012). Perhaps you have heard of Kickstarter, Indiegogo, RocketHub, and Onevest. These are all popular crowdfunding platforms. Business owners can create a profile, post a short video, introduce their project, provide a list of rewards per donation, and upload some images to elaborate. The idea is to create a compelling message that investors from the general public may be drawn towards. Many young, college-aged and below, business owners use crowdfunding to tap resources from close family and friends who support their cause. Crowdfunding is not a reliable option, but it is an option.

Secure a small business loan: This might be the first chance to put your business plan to use. If you contact your local bank or the Small Business Administration (SBA) www.sba.gov, your business plan will help you during your application process. The two most common SBA loans are their 7(a) Program and their MicroLoan Program. Please visit the SBA site for more details. The SBA loan application process is not very fun. Be prepared to put in some time and have your documents in order. On the positive side, however, it keeps more cooks from entering the kitchen. The SBA will not run or manage your business like outside investors might be inclined to do, but you should be ready to provide financials to the SBA on a regular basis when the loan is outstanding. The SBA loan is premised on the health and model of your company and loan proceeds are invested in your company.

Secure a personal loan: Much like the SBA loan above, there will be an application process with your local bank. In fact, the process might feel the same to you. However, the personal loan is based on your health, resources, and ability, not your company's. You can spend personal loan proceeds on whatever you wish. They are not tied to your business.

Secure private capital: If you decide to go this route, you again will need to have your business plan ready to go. Outside investors and venture capitalists will require your business plan before making any decisions. Venture capital (VC) is not a loan. VC is an investment, and as such, VC can be lost. When VC is added to your business model, it opens the door for outside decision makers. Your company will now (most likely) have a board of directors governed by the VC firm. A VC entity might even ask for majority share of your company and controlling interest. VC is an amazing tool but not the tool for most small companies. VC might not even be an option for you until you start seeking the assistance of hundreds of thousands of dollars. When seeking VC on a project of mine, the VC firms would not even talk to me unless I was seeking $1.5 million or more dollars. Big time stuff.

•**Projected Revenues:**
You, as well as any other possible stakeholders in your company, will want to know what your projected revenues look like. Before you take on any possible loans, it will be prudent to make sure you can pay those loans back. You will want to look at your projected sales and/or gross income, deduct your expenses, and ascertain your net income. If your business model includes seasonal or cyclical cash flows, plan accordingly. You should consider all active and passive income sources. If you have a retail component to your business, make sure you include product returns and refunds. Consider your customer base or client list and do the math. If you are ignorant of such figures, online and field research can start to fill in those blanks for you.

- **Financial Statements:**

BlackBull Accounting, or any accounting firm, knows that the financial statements are a big part of any business. Financial statements are not concerned about the thoughts or feelings of a business owner. Financial statements tell it like it is. The three main financial statements (Balance Sheet, Income Statement, and Statement of Cash Flows) provide an immediate snapshot of the health of the business. The business owner (and stakeholders) will want to refer to these each quarter and at year's end (monthly in some cases). Adding the financial statements to the business plan helps create a realistic picture. Financial statements can be created based on projections if the company is new and does not have a history of activity and transactions. It's good to be in the habit of knowing where the company is fiscally so the business owner can detect potential problems or take advantage of potential opportunities. A business owner shouldn't just trust their bookkeeper. They should be familiar with the financials and understand the numbers.

Chapter 4

Who do you want to be when you grow up?

Deciding on the name of your company

When I first started writing this book, I had trouble waiting patiently before getting to Chapter 4. The creative part of me loves this part of building a business. Coming up with the company name, logo, mission statement, website design, and printed material feels like the icing on the cake to me. Creating a cake from scratch is ok, but it doesn't really come to life for me until the cake is decorated. It is the frosting, fondant, piping, quilting, and airbrushing that really makes the statement. Choosing a name is the first part of your decorating process.

When coming up with a company name, I devised seven (7) basic rules you may want to consider. I use the term "rules" loosely. It is my perception that the more rules you are able to accommodate, the closer to the bull's-eye you get. Let's take closer look at each rule and explain in more detail what they mean.

1) Be careful of being trendy:
Unless your business model only intends to function for a few years, you will want to find a name which will be relevant in 10 – 50 years from now. There are some companies created knowing, in advance, they will only be around while a current trend is prevalent. Companies like Cash For Gold and the mall kiosks are good examples. The mall kiosks are chameleon-like. They change week by week offering trendy products with a get-in/get-out strategy. Assuming you do not have a short-term business model, find a name that will

have lasting relevance. Here are some examples of what you might NOT want to do:

Plumbing 2014
Angry Birds Car Wash
Twitter Critters
"Um, Awkward" Dating Service
Selfie Portrait Studios
Twerking Clothing

2) Make sure the name reflects your brand:
This suggestion is tricky but worth mentioning. Perhaps I should have said, "Make sure your company name does not detract from your brand." A neutral, meaningless name works just fine. You can make it mean anything you want. Before Starbucks became famous, the name Starbucks meant nothing. To help illustrate the point, I provided some examples (my opinion only) of names and the potential brand impact:

Superior (Bull's Eye) Examples:

Flour Power Bakery
This San Diego bakery incorporates "Flour" (a direct connection to the baking industry), "Flower Power" (a play on the '60's movement), it is short, and both words rhyme to keep it memorable.

DeadLine Snail Bait
This brand name states what it does (kills snails), the manner in which to apply it (drip it in a line), uses "DeadLine" as a play on words, is short, easy to remember, and opens the door to a great logo.

Central Perk Café
This New York coffee house cleverly tweaked the name "Central Park" (the famous park in Manhattan), uses "Perk" as an obvious reference to tea and coffee, and kept the name short and memorable.

FireFish Restaurant
This Santa Cruz restaurant name has an amazing logo, identifies itself as a fish house, reveals how the fish is prepared (over open flame), keeps the name short and memorable, and uses alliteration to help the name stick.

FactFinders Data Service
This San Jose company collects traffic data. FactFinders is alliterative, spelled correctly (no silly spellings), easy to remember, states the service provided, and can be branded as "FactFinders" allowing Data Services to be the sub-name.

These are a few company names that have struck me as pure genius. When a company uses the naming rules effectively, the results can be fantastic. Each day, I actively look for business names to add to my mental Name Hall of Fame. "Great" names build instant brand loyalty for me. They win me over.

Good Examples:

Iron Sites Gun Range

Sunshine Solar

Perfect Princess Dance Studios

Pretty Pet Dog Groomers

GlossMan Car Detailing

"Good" business names show me that a business owner took the time and made the effort to propel the company brand and image. When I see companies with good names, I give them a mental golf clap. Good names are endearing and give me a sense of obligation to visit the business. It's like a restaurant serving quality bread baskets and passion fruit iced tea. It is easy to overlook the quality of the breads, napkins, and the iced tea at restaurants and cafes. When the quality of those three items is high, the quality of the rest of the menu items is all but guaranteed. This is the impact a "good" name can make.

Neutral Examples:

"Your Name" + Industry (i.e. Mike's Painting, Judy's House Cleaning, etc.)

"Your Initials" + Industry (i.e. MT Printing, C & C Drapery, etc.)

"Your name or initials & Sons (i.e. Martin & Sons, JM & Sons, etc.)

"Your City" + Industry (i.e. Corona Car Care, Vista Beauty Supply, etc.)

Superlative Adjectives (Using words like Premium, Superior, Quality, King, Value, Best, Assured, Dependable, Discount etc. are indulgent. A company should not have to make such claims. The customers will do that for you.)

Neutral names may give the impression that the business owner lacks creativity or does not understand marketing. The business owner may actually be a creative person, but poor name selection gives the opposite impression. I'm not trying to be offensive, I'm simply making a point you might want to consider. Neutral names strike me as last-minute additions to the business plan. They can work but I would shy away from them and keep coming up with ideas. The list above only sites a few examples. Also keep in mind, any company name which seems random, can also have a neutral or negative impact on the company's brand.

For instance, if you named your company "Shooting Star Dry Cleaning" simply because you think shooting stars are cool, the name probably will not translate into effective branding. However, if the owner happened to have Star as a first or last name and happened to be an accomplished sharpshooter, then you might be onto something big.

Generally, when a company is named after the owner, longevity is compromised, it may hinder the sale of the business down the road, the company is in fear of being personality driven, and a self-named business is indulgent. How would you feel about purchasing Mike's Car Wash if your name is Steve? How would you feel as a customer if you ask to speak to Mike the owner, and are told, "There is no Mike"?

Exception: Neutral names are acceptable in the professions of law, finance, and accounting, and in the commercial and industrial industries. I suggest you don't use them, but these industries have made them permissible.

Bad Examples:

AAAA Automotive (cheesy gimmicks)

Cosmic Dust Auto Repair (random, no relation)

Slick Willie Home Loans (negative connotations)

All State Bakery (when you are local)

North Coast Windows (in the U.S., there is no north coast)

Buddy's Burgers (if you offer a full menu)

Bring It! (Names which tell nothing about the company or products)

Sally's Shoe Repair and Purse Manufacturing Company (too long)

I know what you are thinking; there are plenty of companies with "bad" names which are quite successful. I agree with you, but feel this is the exception, not the rule. There are many reasons a company is successful or a failure. The name is only one contributing factor. As a new business owner, you should remove as many obstacles from your path as possible. Why create the hurdle of a bad company name if you can avoid it?

3) Keep it short:

Keeping your company name short makes it easier to remember, easier to print, makes it easy for a client to refer you to others, and keeps the name of your website (and email address) manageable. It is possible for a company to offer products with absurdly long names (remember the shampoo, Gee, Your Hair Smells Terrific?), but the company name itself (Jergens) was short.

4) Connect it to your industry:

If you can make the name/industry connection well, your company may be better off. Working your industry into the company name seems basic but could take a bit more time than you think. Working in the industry can be part of the name or the sub-name. If I were forced to make the decision, I would make the industry part of the sub-name. Here are a few examples or templates for, let's say, a tree trimming business:

<u>Industry built into the name</u>
    Stewart's Tree Trimming
    Precision Tree Trimming

Notice how "Stewart's" and "Precision" cannot stand alone or be branded by themselves? Answering the phone by simply saying "Stewart's" or "Precision" could come off as confusing or rude to a new customer or caller. The "Tree Trimming" would have to be included in the name when addressing customers. This can get wordy over time. The owner and staff might be inclined to abbreviate and omit the "Tree Trimming" in conversations. To do so would be a poor choice.

<u>Industry built into the sub-name</u>
Falling Leaf Tree Trimming
All Season's Tree Trimming

Here you can see how "Falling Leaf" and "All Season's" can stand alone and be branded by themselves. The company name is longer, but it allows for abbreviation. A receptionist could easily answer the phone "Falling Leaf" or "All Season's" without having to say Tree Trimming. "Tree Trimming" can be tagged on to the stand-alone company name. This name format allows for greater brand recognition down the road. If policy allowed, employees at the Coca-Cola Bottling Company Consolidated (true name) would be able to drop the sub-names and answer the phones "Coca Cola", "Coke Headquarters" or "North Carolina Coke" without raising an eyebrow.

5) Try to be clever:
Being unique is a great goal. But I would caution being random or non-sequitur in the process. You want your company name to be clever, not a punch-line. You will want to give people an intended emotional reaction. Giving them an unintended reaction is not the goal. Having a company name misunderstood is a step in the wrong direction. When selecting a unique component to your company name, test it out on a target group to ensure you are receiving the desired reaction. Coming up with a business name that rhymes and/or is alliterative is also a good strategy.

    Rhyming offers a simple way to be clever and makes business names memorable. Rhyming fits in well with the 7 components to naming a business. For instance, if you are starting a pool cleaning service and your last name is Maloo, you can name your business True Blue Maloo – Pool Services. It rhymes and can be easily branded without the "Pool Services." If you need help rhyming, go to www.rhymezone.com.

Strategic word combinations can also work well. You can try these formulas and see what you can come up with:

Color + Noun: Examples- Yellow Cab, RedBull, GreenPoint Mortgage, BlueShield Insurance, RedBox, Pink Floyd, Red Cross

Adjective + Noun: Examples- Running Man, Lazy Dog Café, Happy Clam Bar & Grille, Ugly Stick Fishing Rod, Lazy Pig BBQ

Warning: If your unique reference is too many steps removed from your company's brand, too specific, or too much of an "inside" joke or reference, I would recommend you trash it. Let me attempt to give you some examples of poor choices for a local car wash:

Nanometer Car Wash
A nanometer is the unit of measurement when measuring micro-particles. A micro-particle is 100 – 1000 nanometers in diameter. Micro-particles can harm a cars paint job. Therefore, The Nanometer Car Wash can solve your problem. This might be true, but using this name may create an even bigger set of problems for you to solve. Don't do it. Let's leave the nanometer in the physics lab, shall we?

Super Surfactant Car Wash
Some might know that surfactants are compounds which lower the surface tension between two liquids or a liquid and a solid. Soaps contain surfactants which make them work. They chemically remove dirt from other objects. For those who don't know what surfactants are, this car wash name may seem

stupid and confusing. And I would agree. People want snacks and drinks at the car wash while they wait, not lessons in chemistry.

Death Box Car Wash
Growing up, the carwash owner and his buddies called their cars, "death boxes." It was their inside joke because they all drove cheap "junkers." The Death Box Car Wash may seem funny and clever to the owner and his buddies, but that pretty much rounds out the list. Not good.

6) Make it easy to spell:
Social media and the email industry have made the bizarre spelling of names fashionable. "K's" are replacing "C's", "Z's" are replacing "S's" and the like. If you are going to incorporate this trend into your company name, I suggest you do so with caution. It limits your market target demographic, it makes your name trendy, and it makes it difficult to locate with online searches. I can see a business owner being stuck with a name that he or she regrets ten years down the road as the business owner matures and market trends shift. I can hear them now, "Hmm, it seemed like a good idea at the time." I suggest you avoid going down this road. There are many ways to be clever and unique without naming your company "The Lazy Daze Inn", "Madd Skillz Games", or "Bullzeye Taktykal". Just looking at these names as I type them here is causing me to roll my eyes.

This is another argument for keeping your company name short. Imagine your company "Don't Bite the Hand That Feeds You Deli." What is your website going to be, www.dontbitethehandthatfeedsyou.com? That is ridiculous. Sacrificing simplicity and ease of spelling for the sake of being clever is a bad trade. This also brings up the use of foreign languages.

Using foreign words in your company title might be clever, but it has never sat well with me. I don't want to have to ask what something means or try to figure out how to spell it. To this day, I have never eaten at the Il Fornaio Restaurant in Del Mar, CA. The name annoys me so I won't go there. All it tells me is that the restaurant must be Italian, right? But I'm not even sure. And what does Fornaio mean, fire? I don't know and I don't care. I refuse to look it up. Again, this is just a personal opinion here. Plenty of people eat at Il Fornaio every day, I am simply not one of them. Perhaps the use of foreign words gives the impression of being "authentic." I think it gives the impression of pandering and being short-sighted. I am not a subscriber. Not a fan.

7) Be unique:
When I challenge you to be unique, I am not talking about being clever as addressed above. You can be very clever without being unique. Let's say you are thinking about naming your car wash The Blue Moon Car Wash. You might have a very good reason for that. Perhaps you offer 24 hour service, offer free car washes every blue moon, and your last name is, in fact, Moon. Clever, right? But what if there are five other companies on the block with Blue Moon in their name? You lose your uniqueness. You are late to the party.

You also want to make sure your name is unique to your industry. It doesn't have to be unique in general. Perhaps you name your tree trimming business "Four Season's Tree Trimming." Even though the Four Season's Hotel and Resort chain is well known, you are using the name in a completely different application (**Disclaimer:** This may or may not be possible. Investigate your legal positioning. I am simply making a comparative analysis).

Warning: When choosing your name, make sure it does not contain words that will get your emails flagged by spam filters. (Naked, nude, breast, etc.)

When the health drink company Naked Juice found that its outgoing e-mail was getting caught in the spam filters of its corporate customers simply because of its name, it had to call all those customers and request its e-mail be whitelisted. Naked Juice, which outsources operation of its e-mail servers, even had a problem a few years ago with internal e-mails being filtered out. If you name your BBQ joint The Chicken Breast", you might be in trouble.

Getting put on blacklists is one of the biggest spam problems companies face says Gartner analyst Matt Cain. There is no central clearinghouse to get off the blacklists. Using HTML messages, sending e-mail to the same people too often, and lacing text with typical spam keywords are the major culprits. Often, companies must go to individual spam-filtering companies and ISPs to get their names removed. As listed in #6 above, odd name spellings can also get you blacklisted. Think twice about the words used in your company name before making them official.

What services will you provide or refuse to provide?

When considering your company name, you first need to decide on the services you will provide. Obviously, your name needs to be an accurate reflection of your services. You can't call your call wash "Touchless" if it's not. You can't call your plumbing company "Always Ready" if you don't plan to work on weekends. If you are offering a niche service, perhaps that should be incorporated in your company name even if you intend to offer additional services. The niche service could be the brand anchor. Your "Gluten Busters Bakery" can still offer traditional baked goods, but your niche is offering gluten-free items. Your niche might be based on services you DON'T supply. If your yard service company does not use gas or power tools, the company name should probably reflect that. "EcoQuiet Landscape" might make sense. Once you have decided on your business model and the services you will provide, it's time to start nailing down the name.

If you intend to have multiple income streams (i.e. automotive repair, appliance repair, and HVAC installation and repair), keep your company name broad unless you intend to set up multiple FBNs. If you intend to create multiple FBNs, your parent company can be "The Jones Group", "Jones Enterprises" or "Jones and Associates". This is acceptable as you will not be branding your parent company. The parent company will have the EIN and be on the Schedule-C tax return. With a general parent name, you can brand each of your businesses on your business cards and literature, but can still use one bank account to manage your revenue and expenses. For example, you can brand your appliance repair company as "Jones Appliance Repair" and the bank will accept the checks into the "Jones Enterprises" business account because the name 'Jones' is consistent. These are still "neutral" names in my opinion but could work in the short-term as you are testing your business models. However, it is still a good idea to check your bank's policy or find a business friendly bank that will accommodate you. Banks want your business and should be accommodating. As a general rule, banks can be more accommodating than credit unions when it comes to setting up the business accounts. I recently helped a client establish his FBN. His banker at Chase set up his business account before we had the proof of publication in hand.

Performing a name search

At this point, you should have a healthy list of names you have jotted down and tested. If you can get the list down to your top five names, you are doing well. It's now time to see if those names are available for your FBN, S-Corporation, or LLC.

Filing for your Fictitious Business Name (FBN)

Congratulations! You have finally nailed down the name for your small business. You can now move on to the filing of your FBN (also known as a DBA – Doing Business As). Filing your new FBN is easy-cheesy-lemon-squeezy (my daughter taught me that one). When setting up your FBN, you will work at the **city** or **county** level. For instance, in San Diego, FBNs are issued at the county level, not city. To find the website of your city or county, your internet search will be "your city, + state + FBN search" or "your county, + state + FBN search." **Remember:** you are filing for an FBN here, not a business license. We will address the business license application in just a few more pages.

With your internet search results in front of you, go to the city or county website in which you would like to set up your business and find the link to start the FBN process. **Note:** If you do not already have a designated business address, I recommend getting one. I would not use your home address as your business address even if you only intend to operate a home-based business. This can bring up liability issues, mail and package issues, and can expose your family to harm or duress if crazy clients have extra eggs or toilet paper they are looking to get rid of (or worse).

If you need to set up a business address, I suggest using The UPS Store closest to your home in your city. You can obtain an inexpensive mailbox and enjoy a host of other business services. Your UPS Store address is a real street address, not a PO Box. Many companies will not send mail and packages to a PO Box. The UPS Store mailbox ensures you will receive all of your mail without complication. The UPS Store address provides benefits beyond your business. I use my business address as my permanent address for everything. I enjoy the safety, security, 24-hour access, convenience, notifications, flexibility, versatility, and uniformity. I know of quite a few businesses who use the UPS Store for their address even though they have shops, commercial spaces, and retail store fronts already established. Once your business address is established, continue with your FBN application.

Use the county clerk's office/website of your business address city to file your FBN/DBA. You can file your FBN/DBA yourself for about $42 - $50 + publication fee. You can add additional FBNs for $5 each. You will need to publish your new FBN as part of the process. Publishing your FBN gives local businesses the opportunity to contest your business name. The publication requirements could differ from city to city. San Diego requires that you post your business name for four (4) consecutive weeks.

During your FBN application process, you will come upon numerous publications able and willing to publish your FBN for you. The Uptown Examiner will publish it for $15 at http://www.uptownexaminer.com/. Alternatively, you can use a service to do it for you for about twice the price but without the effort. LegalZoom will file and publish for you for about $99 plus the county fee but the publication is included: http://www.legalzoom.com/legal-dba/sole-Proprietorship.html. Once published, the newspaper will mail you a copy of your published FBN. Now you are ready to apply for your 9 digit Employer Identification Number (EIN) and business checking account. If you have not done so already, now is the time to start setting up some files to keep all of your documents organized and in one place.

Note: Setting up your FBN springboards into the S-Corporation or LLC process if that will eventually be your goal. If you intend to apply for S-Corporation or LLC status from the get-go, you can bypass the FBN process. We will discuss setting up your S-Corporation or LLC in just a bit. For now, we need to address your business entity.

Choosing a business entity

When choosing a business entity, there are really only three main concerns you should have rolling around in your head: Finances, Liability, and Taxes. I will review your options with you, but my intent is not to offer tax or legal advice. I am simply sharing information with you to help you make decisions that you feel good about. When selecting a business entity, you have five options: Sole Proprietor, Partnership, Limited Liability Company (LLC), S-Corporation, and C-Corporation. Let's take a closer look at those now.

Sole Proprietor:
If you are looking for the cheapest, fastest, and easiest way to start up a business, sole proprietorship is the way to go. This is your default position. As soon as you bake your first cake and sell it to your neighbor for $50, you are in business as a sole proprietor. Of course, you will want to establish an FBN, EIN, business license, and a business checking account, but you are in business, baby! At this point, checks will have to be written to you in your name as a business name does not exist. Because there are virtually no barriers to entry with the sole proprietorship, most small businesses start this way. It is very common to take your business for a test drive as a sole proprietor. If you find the business model is working and you have a real business on your hands, you can (and should) convert to an LLC or S-Corp.

Cost and Requirements
- Does not require special registration with the state.
- Requires filing of Fictitious Business Name (FBN) to set up business checking if your company name does not include your name. For instance, John Smith Plumbing would not require an FBN to be filed to open a business checking account. JS Plumbing or SuperJohn Plumbing would require the filing of an FBN.

- Obtaining a business license for your local city may not be required for you to conduct business, but if it is, it does offer some benefits.
- Some cities do not offer both a business license and FBN process. They consider the FBN to double as a business license.

Tax Position
- Owner files Schedule-C for the business and attaches to personal Form 1040. Gains or losses flow to the 1040.
- Income (or loss) is reported on personal tax return.
- Income is subject to self-employment tax.
- The IRS would like to see you make estimated quarterly tax payments. If you do not, don't worry. The potential penalties and interest can be very small.

Liability Position
- Sole ownership of the company is assumed.
- Personal assets are at risk.
- The company and the owner are viewed as the same entity.

Limited Liability Company (LLC):
As you may know, my favorite entities for the small business owner are the LLC and the S-Corporation. When I first set up my corporation, I had BIG ideas. I set it up as a C-Corporation. I created an aircraft carrier when all I really needed was a destroyer. After a few years in, I converted my C-Corporation to an S-Corporation and I have been very happy ever since. An LLC is almost the twin brother of the S-Corporation. The LLC has become more fashionable over the last decade. It's like the "lite" version of the S-Corporation. As a single-member, the LLC works well.

Cost and Requirements
- Requires special registration with the state.

- Has registration and filing fees.
- Does not require filing of Fictitious Business Name (FBN) to set up business checking.
- Obtaining a business license for your local city may not be required for you to conduct business, but if it is, benefits are debatable.

Tax Position
- IRS treats LLCs as a corporation, a partnership, or extension of the owner.
- "Single Member" Owner may still file Schedule-C for the business and attach to personal Form 1040 as sole proprietor.
- If Schedule-C is not elected, LLC will require its own tax return to be filed using Form 1120 or 1120-S after Form 8832 is filed.
- States have an annual fee from $150 - $800.
- Income (or loss) is reported on 1120 corporate return or flows to 1040 personal tax return.
- Your business income will be "distributions" if you are not an employee or will be "wages" as an employee. W-2 issued will carry to personal tax return as wages.
- The IRS would like to see you make estimated quarterly tax payments. If you do not, the potential exists for penalties and interest.

Liability Position
- Single Member ownership of the company is assumed. Multiple member partnerships are allowed.
- Personal assets are generally not at risk.
- The company and the owner are viewed as different entities.

S-Corporation:
The S-Corporation is like the LLC but is a bit more formal and does not have quite the flexibility of the LLC when it comes to tax time. When compared to the LLC, the S-Corporation might be taken a bit more seriously by some in

the business world. It offers a nice array of benefits and provides good marketing power when stakeholders see the "Inc." attached to your business name. It also announces that you have safeguards in place to any sue-happy opportunists looking for a quick and easy pay day. They might decide to go slip-n-fall somewhere else.

Cost and Requirements
- Requires special registration with the state.
- Has registration and filing fees.
- Does not require filing of Fictitious Business Name (FBN) to set up business checking.
- Obtaining a business license for your local city is not "required" for you to conduct business.

Tax Position
- IRS requires corporations to file 1120 or 1120-S tax return.
- States have an annual fee from $150 - $800.
- Income (or loss) is reported on 1120 corporate return which flows to shareholders.
- S-Corporation does not pay federal corporate taxes. States vary.
- You will be an employee of your company. W-2 issued will carry to your personal tax return as wages.
- In addition to W-2 wages, S-Corporation can issue K-1 to owner reporting distributions or losses.
- The IRS would like to see you make estimated quarterly tax payments. If you do not, the potential exists for penalties and interest.

Liability Position
- Personal assets are generally not at risk.
- The S-Corporation and the owner are viewed as different entities.
- Owner must be careful not to co-mingle corporate and personal assets.

Partnerships and LLPs:

A partnership (or Limited Liability Partnership) will involve two or more business owners. This entity is just a tick above a sole proprietorship and just inches away from the LLC. Partnerships seem to be popular when a few friends, family members, or a husband/wife team decide to start a business. There is a trust already between the partners. This trust needs to be protected. If you are going to do something, I feel you should do it right. I would jump right into an LLC if you want to keep things simple while protecting the business and the relationships of the partners. The LLC would not require much more of you than the formulation of a partnership.

Cost and Requirements
- Does not require special registration with the state.
- Written Partnership Agreement should be created. Default agreement might be assumed if no formal agreement is drafted.
- Might require filing of Fictitious Business Name (FBN) to set up business checking.
- Might want to set up a neutral third party for "tie-breakers."
- Obtaining a business license for your local city may not be required for you to conduct business. If it is required, benefits are debatable.

Tax Position
- Partnership files Form 1065. Profits and losses flow through to owners on Schedule K-1.
- Income (or loss) is reported on personal tax return.

Liability Position
- Personal assets are at risk.
- The partnership and the owner are viewed as the same entities.

C-Corporation:

Do you have your Big-Kid pants on? The C-Corporation is the heavy-hitter in the industry. The largest companies you can think of, those are C-Corporations. The C-Corporation supersizes the S-Corporation. With a C-Corporation, the company can raise capital easier, offer fringe benefits to its employees, attract highly qualified staff, and can ensure its existence. But this also comes at a cost. With a C-Corporation, there is double taxation, high expenses, bureaucracy, rules, and compliance. A "small" business owner will, most likely, not ever require the C-Corporation entity structure. If and when that day does come, it would be safe to say they are not small business owners anymore.

Cost and Requirements
- Requires special registration with the state.
- Has annual registration and filing fees.
- Requires a board of directors and bylaws.
- Requires annual meetings.
- Does not require filing of Fictitious Business Name (FBN) to set up business checking.
- Obtaining a business license for your local city is not "required" for you to conduct business.

Tax Position
- IRS requires corporations to file an 1120 tax return.
- States have an annual fee from $150 - $800.
- Income (or loss) is reported on an 1120 corporate return.
- Corporation pays corporate taxes.
- You will be an employee of your company. W-2 issued will carry to personal tax return as wages.
- In addition to W-2 wages, C-Corporation can issue K-1 to shareholders reporting distributions or losses.

- The IRS requires estimated quarterly tax payments.

Liability Position
- Personal assets are generally not at risk.
- The C-Corporation and the shareholders are viewed as different entities.
- Shareholders must be careful not to co-mingle corporate and personal assets.

Setting up your S-Corporation or LLC

When setting up your S-Corporation or LLC, you will be working at the **state** level and working with the Secretary of State (SOS). On your search engine, type in "your state abbreviation + business name search." Doing a Google search in California, I typed in "CA business name search." This search will direct you to your state's Secretary of State website. In California, it's www.sos.ca.gov. Your SOS website will most likely be www.sos.(state abbreviation).gov.

Once on your local SOS site, look under **Business Programs** (or the like). There you will find a link for **Name Availability** (or the like). You will be able to submit name checks online, by email, or by mail. The same goes for reserving your name. Due to budget constraints, some states may not offer services online or by email. They may default to mail only. If this is the case, it will delay your name search and processing, but eventually, you will be able to nail it down. When the name search results come back, you will have three options to consider:

> **Option 1:** If your name is available, you can submit your Name Reservation Request Form and lock that bad boy down.

Option 2: If your name is already taken, you can start the search process over with the next name on your list.

Option 3: If your name is already taken, modify the name of your earlier submission and re-submit. For instance, if the name you really love is "The Gluten Buster Bakery" but it is taken, you can try re-submitting with the name "Gluten Busters Family Bakery", or something along those lines. Remember, once the name is secured, you can brand it however you like. The way you brand the name does not have to be the exact legal name. Gluten Busters Family Bakery can be branded simply as "Gluten Busters."

When setting up your name, if you intend to hold your company as a corporation or LLC, don't forget to make sure your company name ends in either "Inc.", "Corp.", or "LLC." Having the suffix could also help your chances nailing down the name you really want. This will also be the case when securing your website domain. If you intend to operate a company website, you will have a few options when it comes to building your website and securing your domain name. You can go to www.domain.com to check your website name availability, but we will be going into this much more in Chapter 7. For now, you can chill on your website. Let's address the EIN number.

Applying for your Employer Identification Number (EIN)

You have already registered your FBN, S-Corporation, or LLC, right? Ok, good job. Now that you have secured your business name, it's time to apply for your 9 digit IRS EIN number. You will want to have your EIN number for your LLC, your S-Corp, or your Sole Proprietorship Schedule-C tax return. With your EIN, you are able to issue Form 1099-Misc to your Sole Proprietor sub-contractors in excess of $600. Your EIN will also be required to open your business checking account.

Obtaining your EIN (or tax ID number) is quite easy to do. Click on over to www.irs.gov and complete your Form SS-4 EIN application. The IRS even recently started an online application process to bypass the SS-4. You can have your EIN in minutes. Here is the direct link: https://sa.www4.irs.gov/modiein/individual/index.jsp

Applying for your business license

You will want to obtain a business license when you are a sole proprietor. The business license is not necessary if you have established an LLC or S-Corporation. The sole proprietor is "self-employed;" therefore, your local **city** might want you to obtain a business license to do business in that city. Some cities in unincorporated areas do not require a business owner to maintain a business license. If your city does require you to have one, you will need to have your Fictitious Business Name (FBN) and your business address already secured. A P.O. Box will not work. Your city may or may not require you to have an EIN when applying for your business license.

As a business owner, you will need to fill out a business license application. Most cities have a website to facilitate the business license application process. The fees are nominal and can vary from city to city. The application should allow you to document your physical address as well as your business mailing address. If you are based out of a home-office, a Home Occupation Permit might also be required. Once received by business license staff, your application could be forwarded to the City Development Services Center for zoning clearance and calculation of appropriate fees. You should allow 7 – 10 days for your business license to process and be issued.

Can you now see why some business owners don't apply for a business license? They cost money and put your business on the city's radar. The licenses help regulate services and fairness for the city and business owners, but more than that, they provide revenues for the city. Business license fees help support law enforcement, the fire department, street maintenance, disability access, parks, and recreation. Yes, the business license can be a bit of distraction for the business owner, but it also makes the small business legitimate, compliant, and supports your local community. The calculation of your business license fee is done as part of the business license application. You might be asked to provide an estimate of your annual gross receipts as the basis for the calculation. Additional fees, based on type and location of the business may be also be assessed.

If your intent is to dodge permits, fees, and regulations as a business owner, small business ownership might not be your calling. You will want your business foundation built on rock, not sand. Not having a business license creates a liability for you. As an added bonus, if you are a sole proprietor and audited by the IRS, your business license is a key factor in proving the legitimacy of your business and Schedule-C. Your business license can demonstrate to the IRS that you respect the law and have no issue with being compliant. In the event of an audit, not having a valid business license will most likely compound your situation. A license will show you are operating a true business and you are more than just a hobbyist.

Do you need a Sales Tax License, Use Tax Account, or Seller's Permit?

This is not a trick question. In fact, it is a very easy one. Do you intend to sell any products to the public for a profit? Do you intend to receive at least $100,000 in gross annual receipts for your business? If so, you will be required to collect sales taxes or report earnings. Hence, the state licenses. If the majority of your business model is built around retail sales, this is a must for you. However, if you are a service company and offer a few retail products, it might make more sense to work those products into the services you provide rather than being stand-alone retail products. This will cut down on your accounting time and expenses. For instance, rather than an auto garage selling windshield wiper blades by themselves for $40, the garage might provide a windshield wiper "service" for $45 and include the wiper blades for free. The cost of the wiper blade would be a "supplies" expense rather than the cost of "inventory." But again, consult your city and state guidelines and check with your accountant.

To obtain your Seller's Permit in California, simply contact the Board of Equalization (BOE) and apply online. Here is the direct link: http://www.boe.ca.gov/info/reg.htm

In CA, these licenses apply to individuals, partnerships, corporations, organizations, husband/wife co-ownership, LLP's (partnerships), and LLC's. For any other state outside of CA, simply use a search engine and search for "(state) sales tax license" and in .36 seconds (Bam!), your results will be right there.

Setting up your business checking account

It's now time to walk into your local bank like a cowboy kicking open saloon double doors. Throw on some spurs and chaps for good measure if you really want to make a splash. Besides your 10-gallon hat, you will have your FBN Proof of Publication and your EIN in hand. The time to set up your business checking account is finally here. But which bank will you walk into?

As a business owner, you will have many local banks and credit unions from which to choose. Over the last 25 years, I have banked with Bank of America, Washington Mutual, Chase, and Wells Fargo. I also have first-hand knowledge of USAA, Pacific Marine, CitiBank, Mission Federal CU, Navy Federal CU, and San Diego County CU. Internet-Only banks are becoming very popular and are also worth a look. Banks are run differently than credit unions. The high fees generated by banks often go to outside stockholders. High fees generate attractive stock prices for investors, so be careful of banking fees. Credit unions are not dictated by stock price. The CU members are the stakeholders. If a CU charges high fees, they are only robbing themselves.

For my business accounts, I have had the best luck with Wells Fargo and Chase. When I opened my Wells Fargo account, the bank gave me a $25,000 line of credit without even asking. This was a big deal. Part of what you are offered may depend on the branch. I have had to raise my voice a few times when dealing with high fees, but the problem has always been corrected. The fees are also in line with the banking services I am receiving. When you are deciding to open your business account, it will make the most sense to speak to your current bank and go from there. Your home bank will LOVE to take on your business account and will make it sound like their small business accounts and programs are the best. This may or may not be true. When shopping for a small business bank, you will want to consider the following:

- How easy it is to use the bank's online tools (assuming they have them)?
- How many years do the online statements go back?
- Will your online statements upload directly into QuickBooks, or are the statements in .pdf format only?
- What are the business checking account terms?
- What are ALL the fees for services and features offered?

- Are there minimum balances required?
- Are deposits required?
- Do they provide online bill pay for free?
- What is their security protocol if your account gets hacked?
- Do they have enough locations and ATMs to serve your needs?
- Can they process check deposits by smart phone?
- Do they have a branch in your local grocery store?
- Do they offer small business loans and lines of credit?
- Will your account notify you by email and text with automatic alerts?
- What is their overdraft protection policy?
- What other small business services do they offer?
- Do they offer mobile "swipe" credit card processing?
- How is their customer service, phone support, and teller support?
- Do they have a local branch customer service number or only a national 800 number?
- Will the business manager provide their cell phone and email address?
- Can your account be linked to PayPal?
- Is there a minimum or maximum number of monthly transactions?

Having a business checking account is extremely important. Favorable answers to the above questions will make that obvious. You will want to make sure your energy is being spent on building your business and not fighting with your bank. I fell in love with a local Chase bank because the manager is a complete angel. The care and attention she provides is mind-boggling. If I asked her if I could bring my clients to her house for a pool party, she wouldn't hesitate to make that happen. I don't depend on a branch manager when making my banking decisions, but if you land a great one, your life will be better for it.

Securing your business credit and debit cards

Your business checking account will come with its own debit cards. You can request more than one if you wish. Now, STOP SPENDING YOUR CASH! There is no digital record of cash transactions. You will have to rely on your receipts. Receipts work fine as a <u>back-up plan</u>, but they must not be your primary plan to track your spending. Cash purchases vanish like steam. You can burn through hundreds of dollars a month and have no real idea where that money went. You will be guessing. Guessing is not an effective budget strategy. Do you understand this? Are you sure? Good, then stop spending cash, immediately.

USE YOUR DEBIT CARD! The debit card will allow you to pay for business expenses from your business account without the hassle of tracking all of your receipts. You will run all <u>personal expenses</u> through your personal debit card and all <u>business expenses</u> through your business card. DO NOT MIX THEM UP. I recommend putting a sticker or using a hole-punch on the business card to easily identify it (of course, do not hole punch on the magnetic strip). You do not want to co-mingle funds. You will make transfers from your business checking to your personal checking for your wages in order to cover your personal expenses. If your revenues are limited, you can write a personal check to the business checking account to cover business expenses. Always make a memo on the personal check when doing so; that will flag it later on your bank statement. <u>DO NOT pay for business expenses directly out of personal checking or savings accounts</u>.

Some people prefer to use their one favorite, points/cash/reward-earning credit card for all purchases. This is fine, but it requires a little additional work on the business owner's part. If this is you, at the end of each month, tally up each item in an Excel spreadsheet. List business expenses and personal expenses in two separate columns. Total up the columns and make two separate payments. Pay the business expenses from the business checking account and the personal expenses from your personal checking account. This keeps the books clean and prevents co-mingling issues for the business.

Creating your marketing and collateral materials

All right, back to marketing and branding; more cake decorating. After you have decided on your business name, it's time to work on the logo, company motto, fonts, colors, and layouts. The logo might be the most difficult part of the entire process.

The Logo

The logo is a big, big, big deal. The logo is the face of the company; the face of your brand. You will want to get it right the first time. The logo requires artistic ability and vision. It requires an understanding of space, negative space, and the relationship between the two. The logo requires an understanding of colors- what each color means, the feelings colors evoke, how the color wheel works, and which colors complement each other. To better understand color schemes and relationships, grab yourself a color wheel at a local craft shop. To discover color meanings, schemes, and relationships simultaneously, search for a good website or go to www.color-wheel-pro.com. Color psychology is quite interesting.

Like your business name selection process, I would come up with a Top-5 list of possible logo concepts after running a larger list past a focus group. With your Top-5 list in hand, you will now have a few options on how to make those logos take shape and come to life. I have listed three possible options for you to consider:

Option 1- Do it yourself (DIY):
There are some affordable services out there to help you. An internet search will turn up websites like www.logomaker.com, www.vistaprint.com, www.logoyes.com, and www.logogarden.com which can help you. These are template-based options, but might be a good fit for you if you want to keep things simple. These services may or may not provide the level of "custom" you are looking for. You might also consider going organic and busting out your old craft supplies.

The organic approach is a combination of old-school meets new-school. It will involve paper, pencils, eraser, Sharpies, a scanner, and a Paint program or other suitable image editor. Here is your organic step-by-step:

1) Go online first for ideas and inspiration. Do a Google search for your concept and then click on "images" to see what others have already done. You can find some amazing stuff to spark your creativity. You can create something brand new or springboard off something you found online. If you find something you like, print it out to the size you want and proceed to step 2.

2) Sketch your logo (or add to printed art from step 1) on 8 ½ x 11 paper with pencil very lightly. Keep working it and erase the lines you don't want. Use rulers, stencils, and drafting tools if you have them handy.

3) Once you have your logo drafted and all other lines erased, carefully trace your completed logo with your Sharpie. You can use fine tip or regular tip depending on your logo style.

4) You will now scan your logo on your flatbed scanner. Set it for a black-and-white document scan at 300 dpi. If you find too much "noise" on your scanned image, reduce the dpi setting until most of the noise clears up.

5) Once scanned, you can use your eraser tool to clean up all the white fields and Sharpie imperfections. You will want to zoom in to make sure you are being accurate. You will then use your paintbrush and black paint to fill in all of the black lines that are imperfect.

6) With all the black outlines complete, you will use your paint brush or paint can to fill in the white fields with the colors of your choice. Make sure you zoom out to see how your work is progressing from time to time. Repeat this process until your logo artwork is complete.

7) With the art complete, you now need to work on your lettering font, size, and color. Do this in a separate Word doc. It is very easy and fun. You can experiment with all of the font styles, sizes, tools, effects, and colors. Here you will also create a long list of possibilities, test them, and narrow the list down to your Top-5.

8) With your lettering complete, you can now cut and paste the lettering onto your logo page and arrange until you are satisfied. You will then need to save this final complete design into a .pdf format. Congratulations, you now have your "Master" logo. You may have to refer back to this original logo to save into different formats as you begin to upload the logo into various websites for printing, web design, etc. You will never want to alter the master. Always make copies before amending the logo as needed.

Option 2- Do it yourself, and then get help:
As is the case with BlackBull, we did steps 1-8 but found we could only get so far with such amateur work. Before we were able to start effectively branding the logo, we needed to polish it up. You can use DIY logo artwork (do it yourself) for thumbnail images and business cards, but as soon as your printing requires larger, high-quality images, you will need to have your logo professionally altered and improved. Your logo will need to be professionally vectored.

DIY artwork begins to pixelate once the image expands beyond three inches or so. You can see how this will be a problem when printing posters, wall-hangings, retail POP displays, brochures, car wraps, window static, and the like. Converting a DIY logo into professional-grade, vectored artwork should not be complicated for a professional graphic artist. You can search your local junior college for art students willing to help or find graphic artist on Craigslist who can help for an affordable hourly fee. Another option which works quite well is to hire a printing company to perform some work for you.

If you approach a local print shop and ask them to produce some brochures for you, they should have an in-house graphic artist who will "clean up" your DIY logo for you for an affordable rate. This might include "vectoring." This is another win/win scenario. The print shop wants your job and is willing to convert your DIY logo into a high-quality image to ensure they get the job. In return, you receive the brochures you and get your logo art converted in the process.

At BlackBull, we found a graphic artist and industrial designer who was willing to use our DIY images as the base. She cleaned up the images and offered a few suggestions that really made our logo pop. Most graphic artists are aware that creating someone else's image out of a hodge-podge of explanations, crude drawings, and personal preferences can be incredibly challenging. Find an artist who loves that challenge and is willing to be patient and professional with you throughout the process. And don't be afraid to trust their opinion. Most graphic artists today go to school, have earned professional degrees, and understand the psychology of branding, image recognition, color, and emotion.

Option 3- Hire a professional from the start:
At our BlackBull office, we chose this option first before creating our DIY logo. You can search Craigslist for available graphic artists in your area. You can also check out www.99designs.com. At 99 Designs, artists compete for your business for a fee. You don't create your own logo, the artists do it for you. The fees increase with the different packages offered. We did not use 99 Designs; we hired graphic artists directly. We hired our first graphic artist (based in San Francisco), but found this did not work so well for quite a few reasons:

- It is almost impossible to explain your vision to an artist if you don't know what you want in the first place. The DIY approach pinpoints your ideas and vision. The Top-5 list is very important.
- The artist does not share your thoughts, vision, and design style.
- It is frustrating when an artist submits their concepts and they are not even close to what you are thinking or imagining.
- If the artist bills you by the hour, they will continue to work with a good attitude, but your bill will get expensive in a hurry. Getting them to a point where they understand your vision takes time.
- If the artist is being paid a flat rate for the job, the artist will quickly burn out and lose interest if you continue to be unimpressed by their concepts. When this happens, it is quite possible the artist will quit, cut their losses, and tell you to go somewhere else.

- The artist can be very conservative and not want to create a logo that resembles any other logo currently in the market. The artist's idea of "similar" might be quite different from yours.

Professional graphic artists are wonderful. I love and respect what they do. One of my best friends is a graphic artist. The funny thing is, when I asked for his help creating the BlackBull logo, he turned me down for the reasons I just stated above. He knew ahead of time that having him create the logo for BlackBull was a "can't-win" proposition for both sides. He politely declined. If you chose to contact graphic artists, don't be surprised if they turn down your job as well. You might also find the results with 99 Designs are mixed. Because of this, you might want to pursue Option 2.

Business Cards

Did you survive the logo process? Are you now ready to start printing all of your business cards and literature? Good. Congratulations. As you know, printing your business cards is going to be the most effective and affordable method to promote your business.

The business card goes back to the 17th century and tells potential clients who you are and what you do. The business card speaks for you. It brands your company, promotes your business, and lets potential clients know you are ready and willing to serve them. Your business card will let its readers know you are trustworthy, reliable, honest, and credible. It will remind them to call you. Your card can be easily posted on a bulletin board, stored in a wallet, or mailed out with a letter.

I have been using VistaPrint for all my printing for the past 10 years. VistaPrint is amazing. The more familiar you become with the VistaPrint website (www.vistaprint.com) and tools, the more amazing your results will be. I encourage you to spend time on the site and really master all of the advanced editing tools. When you do, the results might astound you. VistaPrint offers so many products; it will make your head spin. It might be your one-stop-shop; however, there is no shortage of online printers. It might make sense to find the one you like, learn to use the tools, and stick with it. The Top-10 are:

- UPrinting
- 4Over4
- 48Hour Print
- Print Pelican
- VistaPrint
- FedEx Office
- NextDay Flyers
- Zazzle
- Overnight Prints
- PrintPlace

Here is a review of the Top-10:
http://online-printing-services-review.toptenreviews.com

Regardless of where you choose to do your printing, here is a word of advice: **Don't Be Cheap!** Make sure you do NOT choose to have the free business cards printed; they will say VistaPrint on the backs of them. Upload your logo, print your cards in color, print on the backs of your cards in color or grayscale, choose good card stock, and make sure the front of your card is glossy. I don't use gloss on the back of the card as I do not want to confuse a client as to which side is the front or back. The back of the card is a good place to make a small note for someone if you need to. A glossy front will prevent people from using the front of your business cards as a notepad or scratch paper. Your business card should be respected.

You will want to hand out your business cards like crazy. They work great, are inexpensive, and you need to burn through them anyway. As you or your business changes (name, credentials, website address, contact information, etc.), you will need to re-print your business cards. For example, do not delay ordering your business cards because you are waiting for your website address to be finalized. Order cards now and re-order updated cards later. Got it?

Collateral Materials and Products

Do you understand everything I just explained about your business cards? Good. You will be applying that same logic to your other collateral materials. When you become familiar with your online printing company, you will quickly notice that they offer many more products than just business cards. As such, you might want to consider ordering some additional items to further propel your brand. These other items can include:

- Brochures
- Postcards
- Rack cards
- Loyalty Cards
- Gift Certificates
- Holiday Items
- Invitations
- Mouse Pads
- Tents
- Bookmarks
- Decals
- Notepads
- Photo Items
- Banners
- Posters
- Yard Signs
- Bumper Stickers
- Branded Clothing
- Flyers
- Cups and Mugs
- Stickers
- Magnets
- Menus
- Labels
- Flash Drives
- Phone Cases
- Appointment Cards
- Car Door Magnets
- Window Displays
- Announcements
- Self-Inking Stamps
- Promotional Items
- Business Checks
- Hang Tags
- Calendars
- Envelopes
- Letterhead
- Fashion Items
- Folders

These other items can be more expensive than business cards but have more permanence. Be cautious when ordering them as they could last you a year or more. You might not have the luxury to simply re-print them as changes occur in your business. As your business and revenues grow, you can start to add some of these other items to enhance your brand and image. The cool thing about VistaPrint is that with each order, they often include some of the above items for free when you sign up for the Pro-Advantage account. All you do is pay the shipping. With your business Pro-Advantage account, you will receive discount emails on a regular basis. Keep your email offers handy when processing your orders. This is also a great way to sample the additional items for very little out-of-pocket expense.

Chapter 5

It's time to set up your home office

I cannot begin to tell you how much I love having a home office. The home office is an extremely powerful tool for the small business owner. Regardless of whether clients or customers meet you at your home office or not, I believe the home office is a critical component to running a successful small business. Every successful business has a "back office." Consider your local Home Depot. The HR department, customer service department, payroll department, legal department, etc. all operate in the shadow of the retail warehouse, but without these departments, the stores would not be able to sustain themselves. This parallel can also be drawn with the small business home office.

How should you design your home office?

The small business owner needs to have a space to think, be creative, make phone calls, answer emails, write letters, invoice, manage the books, handle the banking, kiss the kids, eat a meal, place orders, and maybe meet with clients in a functional but relaxed environment away from a professional building, shop, studio, or other place of business. Your home office might start out as a desk off the kitchen. It might also expand to the guest bedroom, den, basement, garage, or the entire downstairs of the house. At one point, I converted the entire downstairs of one of my homes into a home office. I had six cubicles set up in the unused, formal living room -- you know, the room with the fancy furniture that no one is allowed to go into unless it's a holiday or you have company visiting. I also had two work stations in the den. It was loud, high-energy, and extremely productive. We even had a "shop" cat named Jack. He loved the traffic. As you get your small business off the ground, you will want to consider what you need (not want) in your home office to get things moving. Some of the things you will consider are:

The size of your workspace:
Depending on what functions you intend to perform in your home office, the size requirement could vary. If you only intend to do deskwork, well, you might only need a desk and a few related items. If you intend to run a massage business from your home, you might need an entire bedroom or den in addition to your desk area. You can create a list of what you need and then start walking your home to see which spaces can work.

The number of distractions you can handle:
Your personal comfort is very important when you work. You will want to make sure your home office is set up in such a way that working an 8-10 hour day from home is a realistic proposition. Some people love noise. They let the TV or radio run all day. It relaxes them. Other people, like me, do not like noise. The only noise I can tolerate is the noise I make. Leaf blowers, neighbors, kids arguing, dogs barking, televisions, and trash trucks are very distracting to me. They can break my concentration and even cause my mood to change. (Aaargh! The dogs next door are barking as I am trying to type this; no joke.) Besides noise, you will also want to consider things like sunlight, the view, smells, and temperature.

Sunlight can be good and bad. I love natural light except when it heats up my office or causes glare on my computer monitors. I much prefer a home office in the winter. The office doesn't heat up as much and things are generally much quieter outside. Summertime is noisy. The days are long and kids are out of school. In winter, things stay quiet and comfortable for the opposite reasons. You will want to consider how the sun and heat will impact your home office. If you do not like the sun, you may prefer a room without windows or the garage.

Some of you might also be in the position to set up an office with a view. If your home has a view, and a nice view is important to you, this can impact the location of your home office. You might set up your office in the master bedroom with a vista or the breakfast nook looking out over your yard and pool. A nice view helps some people to relax and think more clearly. Sometimes just knowing you can turn your head and see the world outside makes all the difference. Getting away from the "cubicle" feel is all part of being a small business owner.

It might sound funny, but you should also consider how your home office will smell. Smells are very distracting; good or bad. If you are working hard on a business plan, do you want to be distracted by the smell of baking cookies, a wet dog, a baby diaper, grass cuttings, or a fresh pot of coffee? If so, you might need an area separate from your main home or a space that can be partitioned off from the rest of your house.

Do you get hot easily? I sure do. I don't enjoy getting hot when I am dressed for work. You will want to consider how the temperature of your office will influence your ability to work. Will your work area get too hot or too cold? If you love sunshine and a view, are you willing to get warm if you do not have air conditioning? Are you willing to sacrifice your sunshine to stay cool in a windowless den? Are you able to have the best of both worlds? Should you have a summer office location and a winter location? How will your office location impact your ability to work and impact your family? Do you need to be around your family members or away from them? All of these factors need to be considered so you can set up the best home office possible.

Privacy:
Do you or your clients need privacy? If so, how much and when? Are you going to wax someone's eyebrows or give them a massage? Are you going to discuss personal or financial matters with a client? To ensure privacy, you might need to set up your home office in the den and make it off limits to the family. Or perhaps obtaining the privacy you need is as simple as closing a door. You will want to make sure you and our clients feel very comfortable and secure.

Image:
The image of the home office could be quite important if you intend to bring clients into your home. You will always want your clients to be pleasantly surprised. Generally, a client visiting a home office is expecting to have a less-than-amazing experience. They expect to be licked by a dog, trip on a toy car, see dirty plates in the sink, or visit a filthy bathroom.

Even when a client is your sister-in-law or a best friend, you will still want to go through the effort to make it an amazing experience. Remember, these are the people who will be referring their family and friends to you. Will they be likely to do that if they are embarrassed of your home office or think you are lazy and provided a less-than-exceptional experience? Don't be lazy and cut corners, even for people that you think will not mind.

Quick Story: I decided to sell my house. My good friend is a real estate agent. I called him first. He came to my home to present his home selling strategy. I was not impressed with his presentation. He cut corners on his presentation and took advantage of our friendship. I listed my home with another agent I knew. When I explained why to my friend, he knew what he did, agreed with me, thanked me for bringing it to his attention, and will never make that mistake again.

If you intend to have foot traffic in your home office, give those clients an amazing experience. <u>Brand your home office the same way you would in a professional space.</u> Have printed signs, card stands, stacks of flyers and coupons, etc. When you hear your clients say things like, "Wow, your house is really nice" or "Mmm, it smells good in here" or "You sure do keep your house clean" or "Wow, this looks like a model home", then you are doing things right. Families make messes and keeping a home clean 24/7 is difficult. Consider the mess factor when choosing a space for your home office and remember to include your family. All family members become responsible for the upkeep of the home and need to pull their own weight. The home always needs to be client-ready.

Efficiency:
Set up your office to make good use of space. You will want the home office to flow well. Use as little space possible in the most efficient manner while ensuring your comfort and the comfort of your clients. If you back your chair into a file cabinet every time you push away from your desk, you might want to rethink your layout. And don't look like a hoarder. If you need to set up storage away from the home office to keep things looking nice, you should do that. Storage cabinets and boxes do not need a view or air conditioning. If your home office is too crowded, cluttered, or unsightly, you may find it difficult to work for extended periods of time. This defeats the purpose of having a home office.

Where is the best place to set it up?

Now that you have contemplated your requirements, tolerances, and preferences, you need to decide where to set up your home office. Before you make that decision, there is one final consideration - your family. If you are single, have no children, and live alone, you can do just about anything you want in regards to your home office. The only person you have to (possibly) consider besides yourself is your client. Taking into consideration a husband, wife, children, neighbors, and pets can affect your decision. Without children or pets (and the toys, messes, and smells), the den or family room could be the perfect home office space. However, with children, animals, and all the joys they bring, a garage office or granny flat might be a better fit. Without clients visiting the home office, the set-up is quite manageable. Adding clients to the mix complicates things for everyone involved.

If you do have family members involved and intend to bring clients to your home, you are undertaking a formidable task. Your home office is going to disrupt the lives of those around you and possibly expose your family to health risks. I highly suggest you call a family meeting, explain what is happening with your business, review the pros and cons of having a home office with client visits, and explain how you are going to need the help and support of your family to make it work. Without family support, a home office can be difficult. Your family will be expected to keep the house clean and quiet. This might not be easy. I highly recommend block scheduling to make things easier on everyone.

Choosing your furniture, fixtures, furnishings, and office tools

The time to furnish your office is now. If you do not have a firm understanding of "Need vs. Want", now will be a good time to review that. Your office space (home or otherwise) is limited in size, I imagine much like your budget. You will want to focus on what you absolutely need, before you spend any time contemplating the things you want. When I need or want something for my office or business, as you know by now, I first turn to Craigslist. From there I will check Amazon, eBay, and retail stores. I have found many amazing office furnishings from wholesalers and specialty retailers who post their products on Craigslist. Once I know who they are, I visit their shops and warehouses. And don't forget, you can always upgrade your office furnishings as your business grows. If you do not already have basic office items, you might want to consider the following:

Desks, chairs, tables, and credenza/hutch:
Your desk and chair will be your new best friends. The majority of the time spent in your home office will be at your desk, in your chair. Make good choices here. Function might be more important than form in this case. If you can find an affordable desk and chair with both form and function, even better. Desk and chair styles are endless. You will want to consider what is best for you to work from, and what is best for the client to see. I love open, airy desks; however, I would not choose that design with the client in mind. I do not want a client seeing my feet and all the power cords for my computer, monitors, printer, external hard drive, lamp, mouse, keyboard and webcam. That would be distracting and take away from a great client experience.

When choosing a desk chair, if you need to consider clients, make sure your desk chair is a high-back executive chair. They make a nice impression. Desk chairs can get expensive. I found my $800 executive chair on Craigslist for $150. It's black leather with polished aircraft aluminum. It was a major score. The good thing is, you can get an affordable chair that looks very expensive. You can always add a seat cushion or lumbar support to improve the comfort. A few accessories sure beat spending an extra $700. Oh, and you might want a chair mat to protect your floors or help your chair roll.

I set up all my former workstations with the Ikea *Linnmon* table tops. They were awesome. Ikea also sells table leg 4-Packs for cheap. They look amazing and touch up with a Sharpie if you scratch them. Getting a credenza/hutch is also an option. A credenza with hutch provides a nice computer area and storage.

File cabinets:
File cabinets are not sexy, but sometimes necessary. They also double as a place for your printer, organizer, phone, monitor, or coffee maker. If you need file cabinets, wooden ones can look decent. If you purchase metal file cabinets, I would stick with black. Black looks better and is timeless. File cabinets have it rough though. They get abused. They are workhorses and do not get much respect. They get kicked and have their doors slammed. Unless you are very careful, they might not last long or maintain their appearance. The more they fill up, the heavier they get. They end up weighing hundreds of pounds. Try moving a full, wooden file cabinet. Be prepared to hear cracking and snapping sounds as both the wood and your back give out. It might be game over. File cabinets need to be unloaded before they can be moved. If you can use storage boxes and keep them out of sight, you might want to go that route. Storage boxes are lighter, portable, and can stack. You can use plastic, hanging file boxes if you really want them to last.

Lighting and fans:
Your lamps and fans come into play in direct relation to your office location. If your home office has nice natural light, windows, and adequate air conditioning, your lamps and fans could be of little consequence. If you end up in a hot, dark garage, it's a different story. I can share a few tricks I have learned over the years when it comes to lamps and fans.

I would stay away from lamps that require halogen bulbs. Those bulbs get hotter than a tamale! Many of the stick-lamp, torchieres require a halogen bulb. Torchiere lamps are wonderful. They are free-standing and take up virtually no space. Just make sure you select a lamp without halogen bulbs. When working at your computer, you will really only need a desktop lamp to illuminate your keyboard and desktop work area. My desktop lamp is small and burns a tiny 25w bulb. It stays cool and doesn't shoot glare into my eyes. Installing a few wall sconces is also a great call. Sconces provide great, indirect light, save space, and make your office seem much more elegant.

If you don't have adequate air conditioning or choose not to run the a/c, fans do an amazing job. Of course, a ceiling fan / light combo works great. If you don't have a ceiling light mount, you will need a portable fan. The thing here is, you don't want your fan to get in your way. Having to step over or around your room fan gets really old, really fast. Here is my trick. I have this amazing 10" aluminum, turbo fan. It stays under my desk. I have it angled up to hit the underside of my desk. It keeps a nice, quiet, indirect breeze blowing, and stays out of my eyes. In the wintertime, you can do the same thing with a small ceramic space heater.

Shelving and storage:
When considering shelving and storage, there are two factors in play: Will you be meeting with clients? Do you actually require storage on-site? To get started, let us assume you will be meeting with clients.

When clients are in the picture, shelving and storage become more important. Shelving and storage keep your home office space looking clean and organized. They also provide a convenient location to keep items handy. If you have stock or supplies you need to provide to your clients, those items can be arranged on the bookshelf or credenza/hutch. In addition, the shelving allows you to display family photos, burn candles, have a candy bowl, etc. Don't make the mistake of storing unsightly items in view. Shelves need to be kept clean, dusted, and organized. If you do not plan to have clients visit, you can change your protocol.

Without clients present, shelving and storage is for your convenience only. With this in mind, you might opt to use plastic storage bins to save space and keep the office portable. Without clients around, a credenza and hutch might also become obsolete. Portable bins allow you to keep a few active bins in your office while keeping all others in storage when not in use. Full file cabinets, serving only as an archive, drive me crazy. If I am not using my files on a monthly basis, I will purge them to plastic bins and safely and securely store the files elsewhere. Don't forget to label your storage bins clearly.

I also recommend you stay as paperless as possible. I encourage you to scan the documents you need and store them in an external hard drive. Look for opportunities to reduce your need to store physical paper documents. An external hard drive is easier to grab than 15 storage boxes at 40 lbs. each. Print only the forms you need. Embrace documents in Word and PDF format. Email documents when you can instead of printing them. Once scanned and saved you can shred your original documents. Invest in a good cross-cut shredder to do the trick. Identity protection for you and your clients should always be on your mind. Trash digging is one of the preferred methods for identity theft these days.

Other important items:
You might find your health, personality, and work-style invites various items into your home office others might not consider. One trip to my home office and you will see my whiteboard, glass wall board, bulletin boards, cork boards, mini fridge, air purifier, stereo, boardroom table and chairs, trashcan, shredder, and flat screen TV/monitor. I am a huge whiteboard guy. A few years back at my office in Las Vegas, I traded out my traditional whiteboard for a glass wallboard. It's a 6'x4' ¼" thick sheet of tempered glass mounted in aluminum "J" channel. Glassboards allow the painted wall color to come through. The look is less institutional and warms the office up. Plus,

they clean much better than whiteboards.

A mini fridge, air purifier, stereo, scented candles, etc. can improve your health, stamina, comfort, and enjoyment. My head nods to my favorite Pandora stations when hammering out data entry. Things get quite loud when 311, Godsmack, Slightly Stoopid, Limp Bizkit, Blink-182, and Angels and Airwaves are doing their thing. I use my headphones so I don't disturb the rest of the house. (I am actually listening to Incubus right now. They are killing it!)

Computer, software, and hardware:
The Need vs. Want dynamic is not much of a dilemma here. A good computer and necessary software are a must. Let's break down these items for a closer look.

Computer - Wow, I have been through my fair share of computers! It is safe to say I have purchased 15 desktops and 8 laptops over the last eight years. I really enjoy Apple (Mac) products, but business demands steer me to PC products. I have my share of iPads, iMacs, and iPhones, but use them primarily for personal enjoyment. All my work laptops and desktops are PC. I have made some very good and very poor decisions over the years when it comes to computers. Here is a look at laptops vs. desktops:

Laptops
- They have a nice flat screen monitor included.
- Laptops are set up with Wi-Fi capability.
- I only have to install one additional monitor to set up my dual-monitors (yes, you will need dual-monitors).
- They come equipped with substantial RAM, storage, and a fast processor.
- They are portable in case I need to take my work on the road, meet

clients at a coffee shop, or go to a client's home.
- They have a built-in web cam to Skype with clients.
- The built-in speakers are nice in case I forget my headphones.
- They are affordable. I find really nice laptops on sale for $600 or so.
- I do NOT purchase the extended warranty/service plan with my laptops. A laptop is nearly obsolete in three years anyway as software and systems require updates not supported by the old technology. Be careful with them and they will last.
- Use a laptop stand! The stand has a cooler, multiple USB ports (docking station), keeps your laptop safe from liquid spills, creates more space on your desktop, elevates your monitor to eye level, and extends the life of your laptop.
- Install a full-size, wireless or USB keyboard and wireless mouse when using a laptop stand as the notebook keyboard will be relatively inaccessible. A wireless mouse is the only way to go!
- When on the go, make sure you put your laptop in a padded sleeve and use a laptop case or backpack to carry it. Laptop damage is most likely when in transit. Just ask my wife. A $3.00 bottle of Cholula hot sauce turned into an $800 expense as it destroyed her laptop on one of our flights back from Las Vegas. We did not have a sleeve on that flight. I won't even talk about the time and data loss. I'm still trying to recover from it.
- DO NOT game with your laptop! Do not cruise the internet, open strange files, watch strange videos, open strange links, etc. If your laptop dies, 9.5 times out of 10, it will be because you invited a virus into your system. Your laptop is a tool your business depends on. Treat it well. Protect it like you would your own child. Do not abuse it. If you take care of it, it will take care of you. A system crash is a MAJOR business disruption. Avoid it!
- Do your silly internet cruising on an iPad. Your laptop is for work, not fun. This includes the kids. No Dora, no Thomas the Train, no Bob the

Builder. There are a few good reasons to keep your kids off of your laptop and desktop computers and away from your desk:
- The websites that kids visit bombard your computer with temp and junk files, viruses, broken shortcuts, internet clutter, cookies, privacy items, and invalid registry items.
- For tax deductibility, your computer(s) must be used exclusively for business purposes.
- Computers do not enjoy juice, jelly, milk, peanut butter, and ice cream like we do.
- If children are not destroying your computer with juice boxes, most likely, they will be destroying your paperwork and work surfaces.

Desktops
- Desktops can be less expensive if portability is not your goal.
- Desktops can be more durable than a laptop. But remember, computers usually fail due to the viruses you invite, not because they just crash and burn.
- With a desktop, you can repair or replace individual components for cheap. I do not repair my laptops; I replace them.
- Desktops make great servers if you are going to share software or access your software that way.
- A desktop can help keep your desk clear.
- You will need to install two (2) flat screen monitors instead of one. You might require a special USB hub with installation software. On a laptop, the second monitor is plug-n-play.
- Don't set stuff on your computer tower or use it as an extended desktop space. Desktop computers require the same love and care that laptops do. Make sure there is good ventilation for cooling. Remember to vacuum the dust out of the vents on a regular basis. If small children are in the house, you may want to consider a

childproofing lock for all data ports and DVD drives. Again, kids, peanut butter sandwiches, and DVD drives do not go well together.

Software – There are some software basics you will want to get your hands on to run your home office effectively. For starters, you will absolutely need Microsoft Office, Adobe Acrobat, anti-virus software, WinCleaner, and firewall protection. New "Office" and "Acrobat" editions can be quite expensive. Do not be afraid to purchase older versions on Craigslist or Amazon for a fraction of the price. Also, Microsoft has a new subscription feature for their Office suite of products. BlackBull has access to the entire Office suite including Word, Excel, PowerPoint, Access, OneNote, Publisher, and Outlook for a nominal $10 per month charge. This subscription allows us to install Office on up to 5 computers.

You will need a good database (client management) platform. Microsoft Office should include "Access," which is your database management system. There are other amazing database programs available if you are not an Access fan. I have been using ACT (by Sage) for almost 20 years. It works well, but may be too much for a small home office. In most cases Access should work just fine. Older versions of ACT can be found online for next to nothing.

A purchase of an advanced Adobe Acrobat product may be well worth the investment. Even buying a version on Amazon that is a couple years old is beneficial. Some of the most useful features in Acrobat include: printing to pdf, working with forms, creating one pdf document from multiple files, generating fillable forms, e-signature, advanced security, and the ability to add a text box. The text box feature is one of the commenting tools included in Acrobat that make the expense worthwhile. It's like upgrading from dial-up to DSL. In the meantime, if you don't have Acrobat, you can download free PDF printers from www.bullzip.com, www.cutepdf.com, or www.primopdf.com.

Installing good anti-virus software is a must. I use AVG. I do not like Norton Anti-Virus or most software from Sage or Symantic. It is very demanding on computer systems and slows other programs. Most computers come with Norton pre-installed. I uninstall it and delete it. Find a good anti-virus program. Avast and TrendMicro are also decent. You can perform an internet search for "Antivirus Reviews" to help you decide. You can also add the TrustTool (www.mywot.com) to your web browser to make sure the sites you visit are safe.

I also install WinCleaner "One-Click" on all my computers to keep my systems running well. You can download it at www.wincleaner.com. It is very affordable. Even when you are not inviting viruses into your computer, your computer and hard drive pickup lots of "dirt" during the course of normal business. Temp and junk files, broken shortcuts, internet clutter, cookies, privacy items, invalid registry items, start-up optimization, and the recycle bin all need to be cleaned, repaired, and maintained. Windows based computers come with Disk Cleaning software installed that seems to be barely adequate. I prefer the WinCleaner software because it is more thorough than the preinstalled software.

Your computer should have a sufficient firewall program included in its operating system. Just check the settings to make sure you are receiving sufficient protection and all systems are "go." My AVG has firewall protection. If you have employees or other workers using the computer, it might be a good idea to install some of the other features that AVG offers. There is AVG Family Safety that will allow you to limit sites that you do not want your employees accessing. You can set it up with alerts, time limits, and reporting. It just helps keep the honest people honest. As the business owner and boss, it's ok to be "big-brother" as well.

Hardware – To compliment your computer and software, you will require ancillary hardware items. Your list of essentials should include an external hard drive back-up, a printer/copier/scanner, a fax, a phone, and wireless internet modem.

I get my external hard drives at Costco online or at Fry's Electronics, (including Fry's online). Fry's always has a few on sale. External hard drives are now wireless and resemble "Cloud Storage." This might be the way to go. You can set up the hard drive away from your office or securely mount it to the underside of your desk or behind a piece of furniture. Hide it in your bedroom or some other part of your house. If intruders break into your home (or sketchy friends and family members) you will want your external hard drive out of sight. Note: Read the online reviews of wireless external hard drives. Some business owners complain of high costs, slow speeds, and intermittent reliability.

You can also use online services like Carbonite for your cloud storage (we cover this in more detail in Chapter 9), but there is a monthly expense. Your database of clients and data files will be the life of your business. You do not want your livelihood only on your laptop hard drive. If your computer fails, you will have a HUGE problem on your hands. Data mining your crashed hard drive can cost hundreds (if not thousands) of dollars. You will want to use your computer for data entry only, not data storage. Trust me! Do not be lazy about backing up. Either set up an automatic backup schedule so you do not have to remember or book a recurring appointment to remind you to back it up regularly: once a day, once a week, or whatever makes most sense.

Finding a good 4-in-1 "office machine" (I guess they are not called printers anymore) will not be a challenge. Any trip to Fry's, Costco, or Staples (Office Depot has lost my business) will provide you with a good selection of office machines which will print, fax, scan, and copy. You might want to visit the retail stores, find out what you want, take photos of the signs (model numbers) with your smart phone, then go home and find them online for less money. I have departed from a traditional fax machine and now use SmartFax and eFax. I will explain why in just a bit. Before you purchase your office machine, investigate the cost of the toner cartridges.

I let the tail wag the dog when it comes to office machines. The cost of the machine itself is the least of your worries. Replacement toner cartridges can put you in the poor house in no time. BlackBull goes through cases of paper every year. Toner and paper costs are no joke. We generally use Brother products. Brother toners seem to be the most affordable. STOP! I know what you are thinking, "This clown doesn't know he can find off-brand replacement toner cartridges online for $10 each?" Um, yes I do. I have purchased plenty of off-brand, discount replacement toner cartridges. They have ALL destroyed my printer drums. The best result I ever had with an off-brand toner replacement was 500 pages before it took out my drum. If you know of an off-brand toner that works, please let me know.

If I were you, I would also select a machine that does NOT print in color. All that blue, red, yellow, and black garbage is just madness. Stick to black and white machines. You only have one toner cartridge to worry about. You can get 2500 pages out of one cartridge. If you need to print stuff in color, upload those items to your local FedEx (Kinko's) Office (www.local.fedex.com) and have them print it.

Are you ready to talk about your phone and fax machine? About seven years ago, I finally gave up all of my phone and fax-designated landlines. The only reason I hung on to them that long was for my kids. I wanted them to have access to 911. With the advent of the smartphone, landlines have gone the way of the dinosaur. Even when I was running 10 different phone lines out of my home office, I did not use landlines. I used

Vonage. Voice-over IP is amazing. Vonage is amazing. I saved hundreds of dollars every month with Vonage. Vonage also allowed me to have virtual phones in my San Diego home office, with area codes to support my offices in San Jose and Las Vegas. The Vonage features will blow you away. They include call transferring, call waiting, 3-way calling, caller ID blocking, free international calls, do not disturb, call return, virtual numbers, fax line, Simul-Ring, call forwarding, voicemail to email, and lots more. You should check out Vonage. All you need is high-speed internet. I also recommend seeing how Skype can help your business.

Between SmartFax, eFax, and Vonage, you will not need to worry about a physical fax machine. You will scan the documents you need to fax with your office machine and upload to your online fax service. Other than Vonage, I am not a fan of paying for a designated fax line anymore. It does not price out well. You can set up a SmartFax account for $6.95 per month. My old designated fax line used to cost over $45 per month + local taxes. SmartFax lets you save money, save space, save paper, save toner, stops junk faxes, emails your faxes to you, eliminates paper jams and busy signals, and archives your faxes. Pretty cool, right?

The last two items, your phone and modem, only need to be briefly mentioned. For your phone, I'm quite sure you have a cell phone or smart phone. Smart phones are better as you will want to be able to also text and email your clients. Vonage is amazing, but you might not need it for a while. As far as your modem goes, it should be provided by your internet service provider. The modems now all have Wi-Fi included. It should all be plug and play. When I do not have my laptop hard-wired into the modem with Cat-5 (category 5) cable, the Wi-Fi works great. I have my server PC on Cat-5. If you choose to go Cat-5, you can use your home's existing wiring with PlugLink ethernet adapters. They eliminate the need to run Cat-5 cable by using the copper wiring in your power outlets. Isn't innovation awesome? I purchased my PlugLink adapters from Amazon at ¼ the price my cable company wanted to charge me.

Home Office Shopping List

We have covered the bulk of the major requirements in setting up your home office. Of course there are many other things you might want to include as well. To address this, I have created a check-list of the items you will be most inclined to purchase. I have included some blank lines in case you would like to add items to your list.
(Go to Appendices – see **Appendix F**)

Furniture, Fixtures & Furnishings

- ☐ Desk
- ☐ Desk Chair
- ☐ Chair Seat Cushion
- ☐ Chair Mat
- ☐ File Cabinets
- ☐ Storage Cabinets
- ☐ Bookshelf
- ☐ Credenza/hutch

- ☐ Storage Boxes
- ☐ Trash Can
- ☐ Pictures
- ☐ Picture Frames
- ☐ Candy Bowl
- ☐ Key Rack
- ☐ Whiteboard
- ☐ Glassboard

- ☐ Corkboard
- ☐ Safe
- ☐ Chair Lumbar Support
- ☐ Door Hook
- ☐ Décor
- ☐ _____
- ☐ _____
- ☐ _____

Electronics & Peripherals

- ☐ Laptop Computer
- ☐ Laptop Stand
- ☐ Laptop Sleeve
- ☐ Laptop Carry Case
- ☐ Desktop Computer
- ☐ Internet Modem

- ☐ Phone System
- ☐ Software
- ☐ Small Fan
- ☐ Space Heater
- ☐ Air Purifier
- ☐ Wall Clock

- ☐ Flat screen Monitors
- ☐ 4-in-1 Office Machine
- ☐ External Hard Drive
- ☐ Wireless Keyboard
- ☐ Wireless Mouse
- ☐ Digital Camera

- ☐ Desk Lamp
- ☐ Coffee Maker
- ☐ Mini Fridge
- ☐ Flash Drives
- ☐ CDs / CDRs
- ☐ Room Lights

- ☐ Shredder
- ☐ Calculator
- ☐ Headphones
- ☐ USB Hub
- ☐ USB Cables
- ☐ Music Player

- ☐ Flat screen TV
- ☐ _____
- ☐ _____
- ☐ _____
- ☐ _____
- ☐ _____

Office Supplies

- ☐ Copy Paper
- ☐ Legal Pads
- ☐ Sticky Notes
- ☐ Push Pins
- ☐ Pens / Pencils
- ☐ Paper Clips
- ☐ Rubber Bands
- ☐ Stapler / Staples
- ☐ Hole Punch
- ☐ Pen Holder

- ☐ Staple Remover
- ☐ Candy / Snacks
- ☐ Coffee
- ☐ Batteries
- ☐ Flashlight
- ☐ Tape Measure
- ☐ Highlighters
- ☐ Scotch Tape
- ☐ Packaging Tape
- ☐ Light Bulbs

- ☐ Dry Erase Markers
- ☐ Whiteboard Eraser
- ☐ Ruler / Drawing Tools
- ☐ Office Machine Toner
- ☐ Business Card Holder
- ☐ Correction Tape
- ☐ Tool Set
- ☐ _____
- ☐ _____
- ☐ _____

Printing & Promotion

- ☐ Business Cards
- ☐ Brochures
- ☐ Postcards
- ☐ Rack cards
- ☐ Gift Certificates
- ☐ Loyalty Cards
- ☐ Banners
- ☐ Posters
- ☐ Yard Signs

- ☐ Flyers
- ☐ Calendars
- ☐ Invitations
- ☐ Holiday Items
- ☐ Photo Items
- ☐ Phone Cases
- ☐ Cups and Mugs
- ☐ Mouse Pads
- ☐ Stickers

- ☐ Magnets
- ☐ Announcements
- ☐ Appointment Cards
- ☐ Branded Clothing
- ☐ Car Door Magnets
- ☐ Self-Inking Stamps
- ☐ Promotional Items
- ☐ Window Displays
- ☐ Bumper Stickers

☐ Menus	☐ Bookmarks	☐ Binding Machine
☐ Tents	☐ Hang Tags	☐ Business Checks
☐ Envelopes	☐ Labels	☐ _____
☐ Folders	☐ Letterhead	☐ _____
☐ Decals	☐ Notepads	☐ _____

What if you outgrow your home office?

I hope the day comes when you outgrow your home office. This is a nice problem to have. When your business grows and revenues increase, you might feel the constraints of the home office. When this happens, it might be time to look for professional office or retail space. When securing an office or shop outside the home, you will want to keep your home office up and running. You might move some of your home office furnishings to your new location, but keeping your home office intact will work to your advantage. The home office will continue to provide the benefits on which you have come to rely, in addition to the benefits your new professional space will provide.

When expanding your business, you will need to figure out what retail arrangement will be best for the client, while also being cost effective. You can find inexpensive leases off the "beaten path" or in less desirable parts of town. You will need to find a balance between location, image, functionality, affordability, and value. If you need a professional building, Executive Suites is a great way to go. The bulk of the infrastructure is set up for you. In the past, I have used First Choice, HQ, and Regus Executive Suites. I have also had great results finding executive suites under private ownership. My offices in San Jose and Las Vegas were both with privately-owned companies. You can perform an internet search to find buildings in your area. An "executive suites (your zip code)" internet search should work just fine;

however, driving through the area in which you would like to base your business may reveal a previously unnoticed sign, "Office Space for Lease" or "Executive Office Space available." With the highly competitive commercial market, you should be able to find someone willing to give you a great move-in special. You only get what you ask for, so be nice and ask politely.

Chapter 6

Marketing your brand and finding your clients

Stay true to your brand

When running your company, you will want to stay true to your brand, not true to yourself. There is a distinction. If you can, try to avoid having your business be personality-driven. If Mary (an employee) works at Delicious Donuts, it's great to have customers enjoy Mary and the service she provides, but the customers should be in love with the Delicious Donut brand, not Mary. If they love Mary, what happens when she quits or moves on? The customer base could leave with her. The company culture can be the personality you desire. The culture stays with the business and becomes part of the brand.

If Mary is the owner of Delicious Donuts and the donut shop is actually called Mary's Delicious Donuts, the personality-driven donut shop would benefit with Mary's efforts; however, Mary would still have a problem on her hands if she decided to sell the donut shop one day. A potential buyer might find the personality-driven donut shop to be less desirable. The company culture is more permanent and has more value than the company personalities working there.

Have you visited Wahoo's Fish Tacos? They serve decent food. You will notice all of the window stickers, skateboards, wakeboards, and surf videos. That is part of the Wahoo culture. I'm not sure if the owners or employees are former pro surfers or skaters, but that doesn't matter. The culture is attached to the brand, not the owners. It's a good move.

As your business grows, you will want to continue with brand loyalty. If you abandon your brand, you could lose your customer base. What do you think would happen if In-N-Out launched a broad menu with hundreds of items? Some might enjoy the change, but most likely the In-N-Out customer base would feel abandoned, swindled, or unappreciated. Do not neglect your core customers who have grown loyal to your brand as your business grows and the market changes.

Focus on the clients you want, not the clients you need

When first starting your business, the tendency is to take on every new customer possible. It is very flattering to have someone want to do business with you. You need the revenues and want to help. I'm not saying you should turn people away at the start, but in time, this is what you might be doing. You will quickly find that some customers and clients are better than others. With a retail shop, you're a bit stuck. It's tough to deny service to someone because discrimination laws protect against that, but even service businesses are getting hit with discrimination issues in some cases. If Delicious Donuts says, "Sorry, we can't serve you," they might have a big problem on their hands. If Sunshine Yoga Studios tells me, "Sorry, our classes are all full," it will be much more difficult for me to prove discrimination. If the studio owner does not want me in their shop, they are in a better position to make that happen even though societal trends are working to prohibit this behavior.

The point here is to create the business you want, the business you envision. Don't create what somebody else wants. You can be discerning when taking on new clients and can "fire" existing clients. Create your business model to attract the client you want or discourage the client you do not want. Attracting your preferred clients and customers can be done through your branding, culture, marketing, services, products, and pricing.

Fishing for clients

So, are you ready to start attracting customers? If so, whom? What does your ideal customer look like? Are you ready for the ramp up? Growing a business takes time. The first customers are the hardest to get. Now is not the time to be shy. Remember your business cards? It's time to start handing them out like they are on fire. Talk to your family, friends, neighbors, businesses, groups, bankers, waiters, grocery checkers, etc. Tell everyone what you do. You won't catch any fish until a baited hook is in the water. Here are a few more ideas:

Craigslist – Create seven different ads (one for each day of the week) and post them in series. Post a new ad each day. At day 7, the first ad will expire and drop off. You should keep 7 ads juggling at all times. Do not include your phone number on Craigslist if it is not necessary. List your email address or website. Be aware, business listings might require a phone number. Here is another good Craigslist trick. I suggest posting your middle name for business ads and your first name for personal ads. When a client calls and asks for your middle name, you will know it is business. When a person asks for you by first name, you will know it is not business.

Business Lists- City hall will publish lists of new businesses. You can contact the owners and introduce yourself.

Discount Pricing- If you want an attractive price point, I suggest keeping your normal price where it should be and offering temporary discounts to reduce it. This is in lieu of simply setting a normal, low price. Raising prices down the road is difficult and customers might not appreciate it. It is easier to reduce discounts than it is to raise prices.

Testimonials- When you receive positive feedback from your clients, capture it. With their permission, you can turn good customer feedback into testimonials. A popular way to get testimonials is to set up a Yelp account and have your family and close friends review your business. Some love Yelp, others do not. I have seen disgruntled employees, customers, and competitors slander companies using Yelp. Taking down the slanderous posts can be quite difficult. Be careful. You can also be proactive and create a testimonial form or questionnaire for clients to fill out. Testimonials can be printed on your brochures, collateral materials, and published on your website. You can create a simple comment page and print 3 comment sections per page. Here is an example: (Go to Appendices – see **Appendix G**)

Why do you love (your business name)?
_____
_____
_____
_____
_____

Name: _____ **Date:** _____

Finding your niche

After your "I'll take anyone" attitude wears off, you can start going after your niche customer or client. But whom do you really want? Do you prefer a certain income bracket, ethnicity, vocation, location, level of education, age, athleticism, gender, sexual orientation, lifestyle, or cultural affiliation? Figure out what your best client looks like and create a plan to attract that specific type of customer. Your business might be set up to serve one type of customer better than another. You will want to consider your capabilities and efficiencies. Just be careful while you are reaching out to your market target that you are not inadvertently discriminating against a person who is ready to become a good client.

Salespeople regularly mistake my wife's quiet demeanor as disinterest. When they forget to include her, or make an assumption that she is a stay-at-home mom who likes to shop, they are making a grave error. She is a hardworking, former homeschool mom, now career-minded woman who likes to take in information quietly while forming an opinion. Being wrongly judged doesn't go over too well with her. Keep in mind that even though someone doesn't seem like your market target, they may in fact be the best client you will ever find. Be careful you don't assume or discriminate.

Customizing your services

By simply customizing your services, you can start to narrow down your client base. If your specialized bakery is gluten-free, you will attract a much different (better) client than if you had a traditional bakery. You can charge a higher price point, develop deeper customer loyalty faster, find it easier to brand your business, steal customers away from other business, etc. As your business grows, you will begin to see where your profit centers are. Perhaps you customize your product list based on profits. This alone will result in a 'natural selection' of sorts. Being customized is a careful balance. It can have great upside, but if you are too customized or specialized, you might be vulnerable during market shifts.

For instance, a custom auto shop usually offers custom sound and alarm systems, installation, window tinting, exhaust systems, dash and floor mats, and specialized lighting. But what if that shop only offered window tinting because the greatest profit margin is in window tinting? This might work for a time, but what if a new state law makes window tinting illegal? The business could be in serious trouble. To prepare for such market shifts, I suggest specialization with diversification. You may have already planned for something like this in your business plan. Remember the assumptions?

Find mailing lists

As a business owner, my business model is not built around or dependent upon mailing lists. However, I do not ignore them either. If you approach mailing lists with the understanding that they hold very low conversion rates, you should be fine. A 1–2% conversion is usually the norm. Obtaining mailing lists can be quite costly. High costs and low returns can scare away most cash-strapped business owners. Be careful when going down this road. One way to be careful is to do the legwork yourself and keep your costs low. There is a great website out there, **www.ReferenceUSA.com**, which you can use to create your own database lists. You can only access it through your local library, schools, and universities if these institutions subscribe to the site. ReferenceUSA allows you to conduct potential customer searches by industry, residences, number of business employees, and geography. Your completed search can also include business names, addresses, phone numbers, sales, contacts, and competitors.

Some libraries will allow you to acquire and activate a new library card online and gain access to ReferenceUSA. If your library does subscribe, you can usually find the link in the "Research Resources" tab/link or perhaps in a "database" tab. The last time I checked, users were only allowed to download 25 search results at a time (one page). If you have results containing multiple pages, you will need to download one page at a time.

If you are going to target businesses, **www.Hoovers.com** is another great website to obtain mailing lists. It requires a subscription, but they offer a free monthly trial. The Student Subscription starts at $49 per month. You may be able to get all the mailing lists you need in one month and then cancel your subscription. I have been using Hoovers for over 15 years. It is a powerful tool.

Online searches will provide you with websites such as www.leadsplease.com, www.infousa.com, and www.directmail.com that supply mailing lists for a fee. You can even use the postal system at https://www.usps.com/business/get-started.htm to create affordable mailing lists and marketing campaigns.

Asking for referrals

When building your new business, asking for referrals is a given. All businesses, no matter how long they have been operating, should be in the habit of asking for referrals. Generally, you will be asking existing clients and customers for referrals. So what do you do if you do not have much of a client base? To jumpstart your business, it is customary to pick the low-hanging fruit first. Translation - reach out to your friends and family members first.

Your friends and family members already know you. Most likely, they trust you and want to see you do well and be successful. Once you win over your friends and family with amazing products and service, they will be inclined to refer you to others. In addition to your friends and family members, you can reach out to your relatives, neighbors, and people you bump into on a regular basis in your community. Once you have the friends and family angle covered, you can branch out to professional groups and organizations.

It might be in your business' best interest to become a member of your local Rotary Club, Chamber of Commerce (COC), industry associations, and leads organizations. In addition to your local Rotary Club or COC, there are a few well-known leads clubs such as LeadsClub, ToastMasters, and MeetUp which are sure to have a group in your local area. However, there are countless others which are smaller or private that also might work well. I get approached 3-4 times each year to join a new leads club. Leads clubs are not free. The last club of which I was a member charged a $99 fee to register, a $349 annual fee, and met at a restaurant that required a $10 breakfast to be ordered every Monday morning at 7:00 am. Because my wife and I both joined, the expenses doubled. We spent about $1,000 in meals, $200 to register, and $700 to join. Overall, we spent approximately $1,900 for the two of us to participate. This does not include our gas to drive to the meetings or prep time to shower, shave, and get dressed. Our results were mixed. Some businesses do better than others in leads groups. The most successful person in our group was a hair stylist. I'm not sure what that means, but there you go.

Warning: There are four common mistakes made by new business owners in an attempt to compensate for their fledgling status.

- There is a tendency for the new business owner to be ashamed that the business is new. I have seen business owners act embarrassed and even apologize for being in business for such a short time. Do not do this!

- Similarly, I have seen new business owners not be truthful about the amount of time they have been in business to save the perceived embarrassment. Do not lie about how long you have been in business. Be proud that your business is fresh and exciting.

- New business owners will often act busy when their schedule is not full to give the impression they are busy and doing well. This can backfire and give the impression they are too busy for new clients and will provide poor service. Block scheduling works amazingly well. Try it.

- New business owners can act desperate. Desperation is not the same as providing good customer service. Returning phone calls after 9:00 at night does not convey that you had a busy day. It says you have poor judgment and are desperate. Many clients will not respect your family time.

Presentations and Organizations

Another great way to generate leads is by speaking to groups and organizations as a specialist. You can speak to the groups of which you are a member but also to groups you would like to target as future customers. This is where Rotary clubs might be awesome; they are always on the hunt for speakers. The Chamber hosts speakers too; however, they often require they host the event in some fashion with out-of-pocket expenses and an education piece. You might also want to learn about Career Day at your local schools. Career Day is a GREAT opportunity to practice public speaking with an audience which is not intimidating at all.

Are you ready for another suggestion? Investigate local civic events. You might be able to sponsor a charter school or Little League team, participate at a Farmers Market, or host a booth at a community street fair. It would be dependent upon your type of business, but if these sound like places you might find clients and customers, then it could be worth a shot.

If you want to target specific groups, find your ideal customer or client profile and work from there. If you are in insurance sales and want to cater to teachers, you will want to find out if you can speak at teacher meetings, union halls, and even the schools where they teach. Most trades and professions have associations. You can become a member of the associations that are home to your ideal customer and reach out to your potential customers from the inside.

If this is your plan, do NOT wing it! Create short but powerful presentations and practice them. Time yourself. Know exactly how long your presentations take. I would create three (3) presentations: an elevator pitch, a 15 minute, and a 30 minute. (Note: The elevator pitch can be tricky. I have found it's easier to come up with the elevator pitch after creating the 15 minute and 30 minute pitches. When giving the longer presentations, you will see which buzz words and phrases work. You can create your elevator pitch from those.) Make sure you open the floor and allow time for questions. You may need to hold all questions to the end to keep you on time and on point.

Do not be afraid to NOT answer an overly specific question in a group format. I can't tell you how many times I have had to sit through a group presentation or meeting that consisted of one person battering the speaker with endless questions about their specific scenario with total disregard for the rest of the patient audience? Ridiculous. Do not allow one or two people to dictate your presentation. If the answer to the question is not going to benefit the vast majority of your audience, suggest setting up a time to talk to that person after the presentation. Remember to handle it diplomatically and the person asking the questions along with the rest of the audience will respect you even more for it.

When speaking, create a handout to complement your presentation. The handout can be a summary (bullet point version) of your presentation with your business name and contact information. It might be a good strategy for your presentation to raise more questions than it answers. This can draw in your potential customers. You can book follow-up appointments to meet one-on-one away from the event. And do I need to remind you to have plenty of business cards on hand? You can also bring a nice prize for a quick raffle afterwards.

Caution: You are there to provide valuable information to your listeners. You are not there to sell yourself or your company. Be a giver, not a taker.

Mark A. Torr

Chapter 7

Creating your website and tapping social media

The benefits of having a business website

You are aware that Dr. Evil has his Mini-Me, right? Well, your website is going to be your Mini-Me. I absolutely recommend that everyone in business have a website. The benefits are immense and websites can be extremely affordable. Not having a website is almost as bad as not having a business card. If you don't have a website, you will dread the day a person asks you, "What is your website?" It's quite awkward. There was a period before our BlackBull site went live when I had to give excuses instead of the BlackBull web address. It's so rookie. Here are a few things your website will do for you:

- Brand your company
- Tell more about you and your company
- Share your or the company's awards and accomplishments
- Provide your address, map, and contact information
- Provide a place to have clients register, file share, and contact you by email
- Share testimonials
- Share your industry affiliations
- Post your business calendar and allow appointment-making online
- Provide legitimacy for your company
- Provide positive search engine results
- Sell your products and services
- Disclose your pricing and company policies

- Provide news and information to your customers
- Share your FAQs (frequently asked questions)
- Allow online payments to be made
- Provide a platform to Blog
- Play videos
- Post research and data links

There are two things in business I do not enjoy doing. I don't enjoy having to sell and I don't enjoy repeating myself. My website, for the most part, has removed those burdens from me. I designed the BlackBull website to address the questions I receive every day. What are your services? What do you charge? Where are you located? These are a few of the questions I hear all the time. I have learned to answer them with a question of my own. I say something like, "Thanks for asking. Have you been on our BlackBull website yet?" I then give them a short answer but ask my customers to spend some time on the BlackBull website to learn more about me, the business, how we work, and our philosophy. If I had to explain all of this to everyone, at minimum, it would be a 30-minute conversation. I let my Mini-Me do most of my talking for me so I can focus on the services I need to perform. It's about efficiency and time management.

There are a few industries where not having a website or having a poor website is not a deal-breaker. Some business owners are too busy servicing their client base to worry about a website. This is a nice problem to have; however, if this is the case, having a decent website will make your business that much more impressive. It will show how much you care. Your professionalism will be evident. For instance, one of my business associates is an attorney. Her website is bare-bones. She apologized in advance before I took a glance at it. She knows better. I noticed she had not developed a FAQ section (frequently asked questions). I believe a good FAQ section could do much to sell herself, sell her company, and generate new clients.

How to get your website off the ground

I am not a fan of spending big money on expensive, custom websites. In fact, sites which are more static in nature are now more desirable than the websites of a few years ago with all the "flash" and animation. Flash and animation now comes off as "salesy" and slows down customer navigation. You will want your website to be pleasant, comfortable, and effective, not In-Your-Face. There are free and low-cost options out there that will work just fine for you. If you are broke-as-a-joke, you might want to entertain a free website just to have something, but your customers might not be impressed. If you can swing an affordable, low-cost website, I would go that route.

Microsoft Office Live provides free websites and domain names but your website will not end in ".com." It will end in ".officelive." If you are looking for other affordable web hosting options, you can also check out:

- iPage.com
- BlueHost.com
- Web.com
- NetworkSolutions.com
- JustHost.com
- Register.com
- FatCow.com
- HostGator.com
- WebHostingHub.com
- InMotionHosting.com
- GoDaddy.com

You can pay a web designer to create your website from scratch, but it will cost you thousands of dollars to use that approach. If spending lots of time and money is not in your budget, you should use a pre-constructed template. There are many companies offering pre-constructed website templates and hosting. A Google Search for "website templates" turns up 69,900,000 results in .33 seconds.

Some of the more popular website template companies are:

- Web.com
- Wix.com
- Weebly.com
- GoDaddy.com
- Webs.com
- iPage.com
- FatCow.com
- SquareSpace.com
- Network Solutions.com
- Homestead.com (Intuit)
- TemplateMonster.com
- SiteGround.com
- WordPress.org

You will notice many website building sites are also hosting sites. Some will offer you a free trial and money-back guarantees. The template providers will have a large range of industry categories from which you can choose. You can also choose the template that is best for your type of business. The main types of templates are:

- Web Hosting
- CMS (content management system) & Blog (WordPress, Joomla)
- E-Commerce
- Flash & Media

When you finally select the template which is right for you, plan to spend at least 2-3 weeks building it. It will be an industry-specific template with lots of amazing information, features, and functions pre-built right into it. The problem is that it is not specific to your business. You will spend quite a bit of time customizing your site to reflect and brand your business. As part of this, you will want to create a folder on your hard drive to hold your art, images, and clip-art.

Your website template will have hundreds, perhaps thousands, of stock photos to choose from. Some stock photos are great and can work well. At the same time, stock photos can also give the impression that you spent very little time investing in and developing your website. Would you like to see me roll my eyes again? Watch me click on someone else's accounting website. Each time I see a stock photo of a calculator, a 1040 front page, scales, a stack of dollar bills, rolls of coins, dollar signs, generic business people shaking hands, a piggy bank, gold bars, a laptop, a cellphone, a growth chart, a key, a clock, a puzzle, a check mark….(do I need to go on?), I roll my eyes and shake my head. Really, it's the magic image of an hourglass which is the key to your success? Sorry. I'm not a subscriber. Do yourself a favor. Make an effort to be creative. It shows you care.

For example, if your business is a dog grooming business, you will have plenty of cute and amazing stock photos to choose from. I feel confident you will find more photos of dogs and puppies than you will need. This is great, but those photos will look "stock" and will not reflect you or your style. It might be better to have a photo taken of YOU grooming the cutest puppy on earth. This custom image will show much more than a cute dog. It will show what you look like, it will show you in your professional environment, and show you interacting with a happy puppy client. It will not look stock. With custom photos, your branding process has begun. Such shots can endear your clients to you.

It seems there is no shortage of amateur photographers looking to do a photo shoot. Ask your friends on FaceBook for a volunteer to help you with shooting and editing pictures. I bet you will have no trouble finding a suitable volunteer. Oh, and if you go with a custom shot, please make sure there are no opportunities for an embarrassing photobomb. You know the kind? An inappropriate poster in the background. A doggy who is a little too excited about the grooming session. A messy pile of paperwork in the corner of your office. You get the picture. (Was that pun too obvious?)

You can have a beautiful website up and running for as low as $5 - $10 a month. If you include a "business hosting plan", it will include your domain name renewal and business email addresses. The business plan will cost you about $25 - $35 each month. This is chump-change for the benefits you will receive. Some website attributes you will want to keep your eyes on are:

- Page Limits
- Storage Space
- Cloud Hosting
- Dedicated Servers
- Number of e-Mail Addresses
- Re-Seller Hosting
- Support

When I first started building BlackBullAccounting.com, I was not shy about using customer support to help me get through the learning process. The customer service center for my website is located in the US. There are no bad phone connections or delays and the service reps use email. The learning curve can be tough enough. You won't want to deal with communication issues and international calls from your service members if you can avoid it. Allow for a learning curve as you begin to use the tools and build your site. My suggestion is that you immerse yourself in your work. Do not dabble with your website a few hours a week. Commit to it and get it done. I blocked 6-8 hours a day until it was complete. I did not want to lose my focus and momentum or forget how to use the tools. This was a good decision. After the last tax season, I updated the site and had some trouble remembering how to use some of the tools and features. A few emails to my customer service tech had me solid in no time.

Do you need to register your website with search engines?

To be honest, I am not knowledgeable enough about the search engine algorithms to answer this question. I have heard that today's search engines are intuitive enough to make registering your new website unnecessary. But now that you have spent so much time on your beautiful new website, why risk it? I registered BlackBull on the major search engines. Might as well, right? Here are the links to register your site:

Google:
https://www.google.com/webmasters/tools/submit-url?continue=/addurl

Bing and **Yahoo:**
http://www.bing.com/toolbox/submit-site-url

Registering with Google, Bing, and Yahoo will cover about 90% of web searches. There are other one-stop-shop website registration sites which will claim to register your website with hundreds of search engines simultaneously. In my experience, these registrations just sign you up to receive spam and junk mail.

Search Engine Optimization (SEO)

Imbedding keywords and meta-data tags into your website is part of the building process. They help with search engine results, right? Well, I guess so. But as you know, I am not Mr. Algorithm. I believe 3-4 years ago, SEO was a big thing. But with the new Google, Bing, and Yahoo algorithms, all bets are off. Today, I understand that money spent with firms and services claiming to improve your SEO results is NOT money well spent. I was reading Smashing Magazine recently and discovered an article by Paul Boag which confirmed my hunch. Rather than boring you with paragraphs of SEO related content, I will feed you the bullet points:

- Good web designers and good web templates reduce the need for SEO

- SEO services generally provide short-term improvements
- Good SEO results require continued investment of time, content, and/or money
- SEO companies do not offer great value
- SEO companies do not know your company as well as you do
- Web users can spot SEO generated content which undermines your brand
- Money spent with an SEO company could be spent on an in-house employee doing the same thing
- Optimizing for your client simultaneously optimizes for search engines
- Your website should be focused on good content, not high rankings
- SEO algorithms change on a regular basis
- To improve your search rankings, you can:
    - Publish your own white papers
    - Have a monthly newsletter
    - Have a blog
    - Post case studies
    - Offer applications and tools
    - Include a Q & A section
    - Post research findings
    - Offer user-generated content
    - Post interviews
    - Offer site access to those with visual disabilities

Portals and file sharing

I am assuming at this point that you have visited our website at www.blackbullaccounting.com and seen the "Client Area" at the bottom of our home page. The client area is where confidential files can be securely shared between BlackBull and our clients. This is an amazing tool. Does your business require the sharing of sensitive information? If so, a secure client portal with file sharing capability should be of interest to you. This feature, by itself, can be quite expensive. I receive a great value on the cost of file sharing as it is part of my website package. There are 3rd party file sharing services you can use as well if file sharing becomes important later on and your website does not have file sharing capability. Keep in mind, 3rd party file sharing will direct your clients away from your website. Some popular file sharing sites are:

Large Files

- MediaFire
- RapidShare
- ShareFile
- YouSendIt

Normal Files

- Box
- DropBox
- Drop.io
- MegaUpload
- Google Drive
- Minus
- SkyDrive
- SugarSync

Prices can range from $7 - $40 per month for file sharing services. File size and storage is limited.

What about all that other stuff?

As you research your website templates and/or consult with a web designer, you will encounter a long list of add-on features. You will need to decide which features are the best for you and your business. Generally, the more features you require, the more expensive your website will be. Make sure you weigh out the costs vs. benefits. When selecting your website features, you will want to contemplate the following:

- SEO (see section on SEO above)
- Online product sales
- Online payments
- Research and Library content
- Newsletters
- Calculators
- File sharing
- Multi-Language capability

Built-in content

Remember, we are not trying to re-invent the wheel here. I would be greatly surprised if your website required a feature that was not included in thousands of available templates already available. Good website templates can come loaded with built-in content that will make your company seem current and credible. Embrace the built-in content and look for ways in which you can customize the content to effectively brand your company. You do not need to start from scratch. Capitalize on the momentum your template offers.

Monthly newsletters

Good website templates should include a monthly newsletter. You won't have to spend any additional time or money creating one on your own. When used properly, a well-constructed newsletter can help your business. E-Newsletters:

- Promote and brand your business
- Identify bad email addresses
- Motivate your customer base
- Piggy-back news stories
- Propel your business philosophy
- Generate higher appreciation / response rates than traditional mail
- Keep your customer base notified and informed
- Keep marketing costs down (printing, postage, time)
- Provide a source of advertising revenue
- Encourage client interaction and dialog
- Improve your website SEO

On the flip-side, there are a few drawbacks. E-Newsletters will require a person to provide their email address. Some people are hesitant to do this as they fear their information will be sold to 3rd parties, which can result in spam and viruses. In addition, spam filters can intercept newsletters and prohibit their delivery. With the cost of stamps climbing, postage expenses can soar quickly when physically mailing out newsletters.

Blogging

At this point, you know and understand that blogging (derived from the term "Web-Log") can help improve your website SEO. Search engines are sensitive to fresh and relevant information on your website. But what other benefits and drawbacks does blogging bring to your company's doorstep? Let's take a quick look at blogging pros and cons.

Benefits
- Blogging keeps websites current and improves SEO
- It can improve your writing skills
- It creates a community of supporters, clients, and colleagues
- It can keep you informed of your industry
- It allows you to brag about and brand your business
- It gives you a platform to shine as an expert or specialist

Drawbacks
- The blog-sphere is crowded and quite competitive
- Persistence is required
- Maintaining your blog takes A LOT of time. Re-writing and re-posting what you have already created can save time.
- Maintaining a quality blog is difficult
- Quality blog posts can get lengthy

In my experience, website blogs are maintained when SEO is a concern. Blogs are less popular when a business is not dependent on SEO tactics.

Calculators

BlackBullAccounting.com has 17 calculators available to our clients. They are great tools and provide a nice service to our BlackBull clients and guests. Though they are primarily financial calculators, there are many other types of calculators available for you to offer to your customers and clients. Good website templates should have the calculators pertinent to your industry. Calculator.net has a great list of available calculators.

If you go to http://www.calculator.net/sitemap.html, you will find a list of calculators that include some of the following:

- Financial
- Weight Loss
- Math
- Pregnancy
- Age
- Bra Size
- Fuel Cost
- BTU
- Ovulation
- Resistor
- Ohms Law
- Tips
- Time Card
- GFR
- Roofing
- GPA
- Time Zone
- Height
- GDP
- Concrete
- Marriage
- Tile
- Surface Area
- Wind Chill
- Heat Index
- Dew Point
- Stairs
- Love
- Height
- Retirement
- Voltage Drop
- Square Footage
- Horsepower
- Golf Handicap
- Conversion
- Child Support
- Gas Mileage
- Life Expectancy
- Weight Gain
- Health

Web Links

    Web links are a nice feature to any website. Depending on your industry, your website template should come with some built-in web links. Mine did. A few of the links included in the BlackBull site were useful, but I ended up changing most of them. I would bet you could find much more interesting and effective websites on your own to share with your customers. Over time, you may see FAQ patterns emerge. When this happens, you can direct your clients to web links that will address their common questions and concerns. It is also possible for you to collaborate with other business owners in your sphere of influence and post web links on each other's websites promoting each other's businesses.

    Track your internet browsing used in conjunction with your business operations. When you come across interesting websites, tag them. Bookmark them. You can add 5 – 10 key web links to your website. This will provide a good resource for your customers and demonstrate your competency. Your web links will keep your website content under control, reduce your page count, keep your costs down, and provide a virtual research library for your website users.

Web 2.0, Social Media, and Social Networks

I am not afraid to admit that I was a late adopter of social media. As a busy business owner, I figured I had no time for FaceBook. I felt that phone calls and emails were more effective. Phone calls, emails, and texts have their place, but so does social media. Social media, social networks, and Web 2.0 (user-generated content) are powerful marketing tools for business. It will be well worth your time to embrace these new trends. Your business will thank you for it. This is the current platform for reaching newer, and younger generations of customers. If social media scares you, don't worry. There are classes available for old fogies like you and me. You can find them at junior colleges and community centers and are worth the 2-3 hours and $20 supply fee!

Social media can help business owners make connections, recruit new customers and clients, and deepen relationships. Phone calls, texts, and emails generally maintain a level of professionalism. Social media allows users to "let their hair down" a bit more and reveal more of their personality without compromising their professionalism. Social media chats can build customer trust and fondness. Much like a blog, social media posting can take time. A few strategies to manage your social media can include the help of groups, putting it on your block schedule, prioritize your networks, outsource, and using a social media dashboard.

Dashboard tools are out there to help you manage your social media marketing efforts. These tools allow simultaneous posting and post scheduling. One post can merge with FaceBook, LinkedIn, and Twitter. If you would like help managing your social media posting, you can take a look at:

- HootSuite.com
- OctoPost.com
- FuelOnline.com
- Sendible.com
- SocialFlow.com
- EveryPost.com
- SpreadFast.com
- Ping.fm
- Nuvi.com
- Bitly.com
- Buffer.com
- Tweepi.com
- Engagor.com
- Kenshoo.com
- TweetDeck.com
- SocialOomph.com
- CukeInteractive.com
- ClickWorkforce.com
- SproutSocial.com
- CrowdBooster.com

LinkedIn

Set up a LinkedIn page for yourself. This will serve as your resume. Your customers, clients, and fellow professionals might like to know more about you. A potential customer will know that your business literature or website might only reveal a portion of your capabilities, character, and background. It can come off as rude when a potential client asks about your background. In essence, they are saying, "prove it," when asking about your qualifications. When you are in the position to offer your LinkedIn page for a client to review, it can be disarming. Make sure you include a web link to your LinkedIn page on your business website.

LinkedIn can be searched to find a specific talent or skill set. It is fair for you to state your qualifications without feeling boastful. You can also form or join LinkedIn groups. These groups can be a good platform to promote your business.

One of my better clients did a LinkedIn "background" check on me before becoming a BlackBull client. Our face-to-face interview went just fine. She simply wanted to check out and verify my credentials before entrusting her personal taxes, business taxes, and bookkeeping to me. She admitted this to me after the fact. Most likely, you will never know who verifies your credibility on LinkedIn or how many clients you land because of it. You also may never know how many clients you lose because you do not have a LinkedIn profile.

Facebook, Twitter, and YouTube

If you choose to use social media management, you can post on all of your social media outlets simultaneous with one post. You also should look at creating a Facebook page exclusively for your business. When relevant news is worthy of posting, it is nice to have a business-designated page to do that. Facebook and Twitter are informal, unlike LinkedIn, which is geared toward business. With your Facebook page, you have a good platform to reach out to friends, family, neighbors, community groups, alumni, and grade school friends. A few good posts can generate interest in your new business and be a decent lead generation source. Referrals come naturally on social media sites.

If you intend to blog and/or have relevant findings and information, don't forget to add the links to your blog or include interesting articles in your Facebook posts. With Twitter, your micro-blogging "tweets" are quick and effective. With a 140-character limit, you are forced to get to the point and move on. Using key words is more prevalent with Twitter and set off with hashtags. Because Twitter has character limitations, links can sometimes be too long to post. If this is the case, you will need to use tools to shorten your links. Try using the following:

- http://bit.ly
- www.tinyurl.com

Both of these link-reducing tools work fine. With Bit.ly, you will also have a tracking feature that captures how many people clicked on your link. This might be nice if you are concerned about the relevance of your posted topics.

YouTube is an amazing tool. Whenever I need to perform a repair on my cars or motorcycles, I just YouTube it. Voilà, the how-to video shows right up. It's awesome. Businesses often post such videos to help their potential customers and keep them informed. Videos are a great way to establish credibility for you and your business as authorities and industry leaders. Posting a video also gives you another excuse to post your video link on Facebook and Twitter. Infomercial-style videos are effective when professionally done.

Be careful of what you post. Remember, you are branding your company. First impressions matter. Your video will convey your company culture. Do you want to look like you are recording in Mom's basement? Are you trying to look like Wayne's World? Be aware of your surroundings. Make your background look professional. If you spend a few bucks, you can take your raw footage to a videographer and have it edited into a quality video with some production value. If you want to get your hands dirty, you can use Microsoft PowerPoint or Publisher to create your custom videos to leave a nice impression with your viewers. Adding some background music is a nice touch.

Professional Organizations, Groups, and Forums

How do you feel about speaking in public? Are you glossophobic? If you don't mind public speaking, it might be worth pursuing. Since most people are afraid of it, you will gain instant credibility and respect when you take the mic. This will say much about you as a person regardless of what you have to say or what services you have to offer. If you are brave enough to stand up to public scrutiny, you will, most likely, be qualified to handle your client's challenges in their minds. Public speaking offers an amazing opportunity. Not only can you demonstrate your prowess, but you can also convey your personality and sense of humor. You will have the chance to endear people to you regardless of the content about which you are speaking. A bit of research will uncover the local groups and organizations in your area, including leads groups. If you decide to join a group(s) to facilitate lead generation for your business, you will now have the opportunity to speak to your peers.

Are you still afraid of public speaking? I get it. Fortunately, you can do lots of group speaking without having to open your mouth or stand up in front of anyone. Use your keyboard instead. Type your blogs and articles. Post them to your social media sites and the new groups you have discovered. Be sure to include your name, credentials, business name, and contact information including the link to your website. When posting and responding to posts, be careful. Here are a few tips to keep you on track:

- Be confident but not arrogant
- Exercise humility
- Do not be critical of others
- Be careful of being absolute. Leave room to wiggle out of a corner
- Separate the facts from your opinions
- Do not be judgmental
- Be complimentary
- Use humor when possible
- Mix in some self-deprecation

If you do have a fear of public speaking and would like to attempt to overcome it, here are a few tips on how to do that:

Identify your fear - In reality, it is not a fear of speaking, but a fear of being judged that we fret over. We fear making a mistake. You know how to speak. Just relax and deliver your message.

Don't fret – Your listeners admire you for being up there, respect you, and want to see you succeed. Remember, they are nervous too. Some in the group will offer you positive feedback to encourage you. You will see head nods and smiles. Focus on those people and avoid focusing on the guy grimacing at you.

Prepare – There is no substitute for being prepared. You know this. Start off with small presentations of only a few bullet points. Once your comfort level grows, you can include more content. Know your material and practice in a mirror and in front of family and/or friends. You can also video yourself and analyze the playback for things you did correctly or things you can improve. I discovered in videos of me surfing that my arms waved horribly and my right hand would bend back like it was broken. It looked horrible. I changed my style as a result. You should also create and follow a printed handout. Pass it out in advance and just follow the bullet points as you go. The handout will keep your listeners engaged and keep some of the attention off you. Don't use fillers. Don't say "um" or "like". If you hit a dead spot, that's fine. Stay silent. Collect your thoughts and resume. That shows poise. Saying "um" shows fear. Silence is very powerful.

Enjoy the experience – Flip the dynamic. Rather than fear your presentation, enjoy it. Breathe and relax. Engage in small talk with some group members beforehand to loosen up. Learn a few names. Develop a few friendly faces. Tell them you are nervous. They will encourage you. You can call on or refer to those group members as you speak. This will keep you and the crowd loose, divert the group's attention, and pull the audience in. If you are nervous and your hands are shaking, hold something sturdy like a clipboard or book. Don't hold a single sheet of paper as it will flutter, make noise, and exaggerate your hand twitch. Laugh and smile. This is a natural stress reliever. Start with an industry joke to loosen up the group. Tell a story to make a point. Audiences love stories and you can't screw them up. Ask questions. When you ask a question and pause, it puts the pressure on the group and off of you (for a bit). Don't hunch. Stand tall. Own your space. Plan ahead of time for members of the group to yawn, look at their watch, tap a pen, etc. Don't be distracted. You are not trying to convince 100% of your listeners you are amazing, just the potential clients in that group. Remember, you don't want "yawning guy" to be your client anyway.

When giving a group presentation, or even when posting in a blog, it is doubtful you will have sufficient time to offer comprehensive solutions to the topics or questions of the day. That's fine. The point of the presentation or blog is to open up, provide information, and establish a dialogue between you and your potential clients. Those who value your help will seek you out and ask for more of your time. That is the goal. Stimulate interest and create a follow-up plan.

Chapter 8

Can you afford all of this?

This is a question you will want to ask yourself. You will want to pool your resources to see where you stand. You have some decisions to make but those decisions need to be informed. Now is not the time to use hope as a strategy. You need facts. You will want to know the following:

- How much cash do you have on hand?
- What credit lines are available to you?
- What are your billing rates and fees going to be?
- How much time is your new business going to involve?
- What is the size of your current client or customer base?
- What are your current monthly revenues?
- What are your current monthly expenses?
- What are your new expenses going to be?
- Do you need to keep your day job and phase into your new business or can you afford to jump in with both feet?
- Do you have the time to run your business?
- Can your family adjust?
- What demands are going to be thrust upon you?

Be realistic as you address these questions. Keep good notes. Update your notes and refer to them often. Other than marriage, children, buying a house, and getting a full-face tattoo, starting a new business will be one of the most important decisions you will ever make. Please don't forget, time and money are both in play here. You need to manage both well. Let's take a closer look at your time and money variables.

Start-Up costs

Your start-up costs will vary depending on the nature of your business and your risk tolerance. Chapters 4, 5 and 7 address most of your start-up costs. Please refer back to them and have your spreadsheet ready. It's time to start crunching the numbers. You will need to decide what you want your new business to look like. This will have a direct impact on your expenses. As you know, it will not cost as much to run a yoga studio out of your back yard as it would to rent a commercial space in your local shopping center. Starting out in a home office is your most economical option; expenses increase from there.

What rates should you charge?

Another great question. In general, your rates will be attractive when you are first starting out to entice new customers and clients. Remember to discount your higher normal fees rather than having a low standard fee. It is much easier to reduce discounts than it is to raise your standard fees. Do your homework. Find out what the industry is charging and set your price accordingly based on your facilities, education, and certifications. The busier you get, the more you can charge. This is a tricky balance so be careful.

You will need to look at your current (family) income and expenses and determine what kind of revenues you need to see in order to make ends meet. You may need to keep your day job and work your new business on evenings and weekends until momentum and revenues build. If you have a spouse and children you are supporting, your ramp-up timeline could be impacted. At the same time, perhaps your spouse and children can contribute to your new business start-up and relieve some of your stress. These are conversations you will need to have with your family members. When building your business, there are plenty of things you can do before you actually open your doors to new customers. Make sure all of the groundwork is done first. Do all you can from Chapters 4, 5, and 7 before you actually start spending time with clients and customers. These administrative tasks can be done after-hours and on weekends while you still have a day job.

Should you use a loss leader in your billing and pricing practice?

Uh oh. Are we in the office of Redundancy? I believe we have spoken about your billing rates two other times at this point. I don't want to be repetitious, but I want to make a point here. You may want to incorporate a "loss leader" into your products or services. A loss leader, according to Investopedia, is

> "A business strategy in which a business offers a product or service at a price that is not profitable for the sake of offering another product/service at a greater profit or to attract new customers. This is a common practice when a business first enters a market; a loss leader introduces new customers to a service or product in the hope of building a customer base and securing future recurring revenue."

Does that make sense? For instance, have you ever wondered why Discount Tire offers free flat repair, or why Data Doctors offers free laptop check-ups, or why some buffets allow children to eat for free? These are all loss leaders. They attract new customers, get them in the door, get them into their database, help create a "drip" campaign, and upsell them on other products and services. This strategy works very well. You may want to consider using it when ramping up your business.

LEGOLAND is down the street from my house. Children under three are admitted into the park for free. Again, this is a loss leader. LEGOLAND knows that the parents of a two year old are not going to push him through the turnstiles with their diaper bag and say, "Have a great day, honey. We'll be back to get you at 5:00." The parents will purchase at least one ticket for $85 to take advantage of the "free" children's ticket. Mix in lunch at Burger Stop, Castle Burgers, Knight's Table BBQ, or Pizza Mania (yes, I have eaten at all of these restaurants) and your "free" kids ticket will cost you another $40 - $50 in food. So much for free, right? To this day, whenever I hear a business claim "kids are free", I chuckle and roll my eyes. My hat's off to LEGOLAND. They get it. They exploit it. Good for them.

Loss leaders are a great strategy if you play them right. You will want to <u>strike a balance</u> between offering a product or service with enough value to lure new customers to you while, at the same time, maintaining profitability in your business. Your business should not suffer as a result. The outcome should always be positive. For instance, H&R Block offered free simple tax returns a few years ago to get new customers in the door. The loss leader worked at getting new customers in the door but the company ended up losing millions of dollars that year. The short-term and long-term pay-offs never materialized. To make things worse, Block staff was forced to burn their time doing tax returns for free. The HRB staff lost wages and office morale declined. It was a lose/lose situation for Block. The only ones to win here were the people getting their tax returns completed for free.

You may need to try out different loss leaders if you are going to implement this strategy. Here are a few examples to help you wrap you head around the loss leader concept.

Poor Examples

Too Costly:
- Free Big Gulps
- Free burrito plate
- Free oil change
- Free dinner
- Free tax return
- Free dozen donuts

No Value:
- Free sticker
- Free candy
- Free branded item
- Free stick of gum
- Free bottle of water
- Free desk calendar

Too Random:
- Free light bulb
- Free screwdriver
- Free picture frame

Possible Examples

- Free gift cards
- Free iPad drawing
- Free admission
- Free inspections
- Free estimates
- Free installation

Good Examples

- 3 months free rent
- Inexpensive up-sizing
- 1 hour free instruction
- Free class
- Free fish taco
- Free 12 oz. soft drinks for a limited time
- 1 month free membership with sign-up
- Free coffee with breakfast burrito
- Free one-room carpet cleaning
- Free small popcorn with ticket

- Free refills
- Free kids' meal
- Free 24-hour pass
- Free checking
- Free donut hole
- Free yoga mat with membership
- Free oil change with set of tires
- Free carwash with gas purchase
- Free drink with meal purchase
- Free bag of chips with meal

(**Note:** See how adding conditions can convert a bad example into a good one?)

If you are a fan of psychology, you will recall that people have a natural aversion to things that are free or too deeply discounted. Accepting handouts or free items does not benefit the self-worth of the person receiving it. Accepting free items unconditionally makes a person feel bad about them self. Self-respecting individuals want to earn their keep and pay for their items. This is why, if you hang a sign outside your donut shop that reads "Free Donuts", you will not attract the customers you desire. Most likely, you will attract those who do not earn an income or have low moral character. I can envision adolescents lining up at your door after school. Your new customers will not support your business or help it grow. However, if your sign reads "Buy 10 get 2 Free", you will have dramatically different results.

A quality customer will be quite comfortable with being "rewarded" for their patronage. The two free donuts are no longer charity; they are a "thank you." Again, the word "free" can be quite powerful with both positive and negative connotations. In many cases, a "discount" might be a better angle to achieve your goal. The two terms are synonymous when it comes to your bookkeeping, but they offer a different perceived reality.

If you are not aware of the phrase *"**If something seems too good to be true, it probably is**"*, now you are. This is a good rule to follow. Say for instance you saw a coupon for a free oil change. What would you be thinking? Would you think, "This is awesome! I get a great oil change and save $40 in the process?" Or would you think, "Um, a free oil change? Are they going to use the correct oil or even replace my filter? This sounds sketchy. Is this going to be bad for my car?" I personally would feel that cashing in that coupon for a free oil change would be taking a risk. I would not do it. I would much rather have a coupon for $10 off than for free. Consumer studies have shown that many people feel that free = not worth anything.

Let's look at our donuts again. Are the two free donuts actually free? Of course not. Not according to the business books. For your business, the two free donuts simply represent a discount to a normally priced box of a dozen donuts. You are simply printing the word free on your sign instead of the word discount. This is why I am recommending you play with your discounts and loss leaders. See which approach gets you the best results. One free personal training session might not work as well as 30% off your first three personal training sessions. Or, the inverse could be true. Keep your mind open and see what works in your industry. In the course of my research, I discovered an article printed by Ideas4SmallBiz.com making an argument in favor of free giveaways. Here are six reasons why you might like to give away free items or services.

1) **Free stuff creates a buzz** - In today's day and age, it doesn't take long for news to travel. Facebook posts and tweets about free offers can spread fast. Readers might be more willing to pay more attention if they hear something from a friend.

2) **Free stuff offers risk-free sampling** - This is a benefit if you want to prove that you have something different or better to offer. People are more likely to try something they normally wouldn't if it is free and without

commitment. Have any of you seen me at Costco on Saturdays and Sundays? I can be found mowing through the free samples carts like Koi fish attacking pellets in a pond. The energy bar pieces don't stand a chance with me around.

3) Free stuff hooks customers to spend more - Sure, there's always a few that will order the bare minimum and leave. But most will stay for a while and order more.

4) Customers are more forgiving when something is free - Free items and services can be an advantage for a new business trying to work out the kinks. While the employees struggle to learn the ropes, figure out the new computer system and adjust to the learning curve, you have a set of customers who are a little more willing to go with the flow. Just don't take advantage of them. If they leave with a negative perception, they may never come back. You may need to consider adding "for a limited time."

5) Free stuff promotes your brand - Customers remember how special they felt and think highly of you. It's also about positioning. Sometimes offering a completely FREE appetizer is more appealing to a guest than 15% off their meal, even though the percentage discount might be an actual greater dollar amount. People perceive that they're getting something for nothing, which makes them giddy. (Or the inverse – be careful.)

6) Free stuff creates a buying habit - By offering something free, people are more likely to give your business a try. And once they've tried it, assuming the experience was positive, they're more likely to come back. We all know it's harder to gain a new customer than keep a current one and that buyers are creatures of habit. They go with what they know and feel comfortable with. Part of the challenge of a new business, or even an established business, is driving traffic (foot traffic to a retail location or traffic to your website). So now that your location is part of their consideration set, you're much more likely to gain their repeat business in the future.

You can see the entire article at http://ideas4smallbiz.com/2012/04/6-reasons-giving-away-free-stuff-can-work-for-your-small-business/.

How should you collect your fees and accounts receivable?

If you have a retail or storefront presence, collecting your fees is not a difficult proposition. It's a "no cash - no deal" proposition. Customers pay-on-demand or pre-pay. I would not allow establishing lines of credit or paying at a later time. The Wimpy, "I will gladly pay you Tuesday for a hamburger today," approach does not work. (For the record, Popeye is awesome.) This could set a bad precedent. If you are a service business, much of the same will apply but there will be the opportunity to bill or invoice your customers after the work is complete.

Make sure you are set up to accept credit cards. Two of the most brilliant tools you can have for your business or home office are the iPhone Square or the PayPal Triangle card swipers. There is also the Intuit GoPayment product, but I am not as familiar with it (http://payments.intuit.com/mobile-credit-card-processing/). You, of course, can have the larger, desktop card units seen at retail stores and convenience stores, but those machines can require expensive, long-term contracts. Credit card processing companies want to lease credit card machines with extended, binding contracts. If your business slows down or you close its doors, too bad. You are stuck paying the remainder of your contract. Your local bank will also offer card swipers as part of their business banking services, but they still come with fees. Once the PDA plug-in units came around, I moved away from my desktop units and have not gone back.

The Square gives you two options: The Square Stand and the Square Reader. You can read more about them online at **www.squareup.com**.
The Square Stand looks astounding and works brilliantly. It is a complete desktop POS (point of sale) system that works with your iPad. It only costs $99. By now, you have probably seen the Square Stand at your local retail shops. The Square Reader is a mobile swiper which plugs right in to your smartphone earbud jack. It allows you to process credit cards from anywhere. Your customer signs with their finger on your smartphone. The Square Reader costs...Oh, that's right, it's free! It's truly amazing. Both options only charge a vendor fee of 2.75%. This is less than the expensive desktop versions. Some of the Square benefits include:

- Accepting all payments, even without a connection
- Sending receipts via email, text message, or printing them out
- Collecting customer feedback from digital receipts
- Printing or emailing sales reports
- Adjusting taxes, tipping, and discounts
- Managing inventory in real time
- Accepting orders online for pickup in person
- Creating employee logins

The PayPal Swiper is virtually identical to the Square but only charges a 2.7% fee. You also receive live customer support, cash back, and do not have any long-term contracts or commitments. At BlackBull, we use the PayPal Triangle swiper. As an added bonus, PayPal also offers small business "Working Capital" loans with relative ease as a PayPal subscriber. Learn more about the PayPal loans at:
https://www.paypal.com/webapps/workingcapital/

Here is a PayPal Swipe comparison:

PayPal Comparison

	PayPal	Intuit GoPayment	Square
App and card reader for credit card payments	✓	✓	✓
Flexible multi-user settings	✓	✓	✓
Live customer support	✓	✓	✗
Accept PayPal payments, record cash and check payments, plus email invoices	✓	✗	✗
Comes with debit card with 1% cash back on eligible purchases	✓	✗	✗
Access funds in minutes	✓	✗	✗
Pricing*	2.7%	varies	2.75%

*Excluding keyed-in and scanned credit card transactions.   (Image courtesy of PayPal)

You can read more about the PayPal swiper at:
https://www.paypal.com/webapps/mpp/credit-card-reader

In a service industry, you can collect a portion up front and the balance upon completion, or simply invoice the client for all the fees upon completion. At BlackBull, we either collect when work is completed (like we do when completing a tax return) or we invoice after work has been completed (as is the case with our bookkeeping). We do not normally collect a portion of our fees up front and bill for the balance later like a plumber or carpet installer.

Many of my clients are on a case-by-case basis. Some of my clients are better than others so they might receive better terms. Client loyalty and/or history is a factor. The greater the client history, the greater the tendency to be more lenient in your billing practice. Just remember, if you allow payment terms, it's not a matter of "if" but "when" someone will take advantage of you. When others owe you money, there will always be those who let you down and stiff you. If you know this going in, it will take the sting out of it. When you grant terms or offer flexibility on your payments, know that you are rolling the dice. If you are going to allow payment terms, set dollar limits and time limits to help regulate your accounts receivable. You may need to monitor your billing and accounts receivable closely.

Tracking your time and mileage

For some reason, many business owners don't respect their own time. I have seen business owners scold their own children and family members for not being sensitive to their time, while allowing their clients and customers to walk all over them and treat them like dirty dogs. I don't understand this imbalance and recommend against it. It's perfectly normal to respect your customers while demanding their respect in return. Again, block schedule.

Track the time you spend on running your business. Treat your time like money. See where it goes. You will want to manage your time as much as you manage your finances. The two go hand-in-hand. This includes your time spent driving. Make sure you track your time and mileage spent on business operations. I use the MileBug app in my iPhone (check for MileBug in your phone app store or go to www.milebug.com). MileBug will track all of your trips, time, and mileage and can email you Excel spreadsheets on the data. It's awesome. You will need your mileage data come tax time. The MileBug app can:

- Track your full path with GPS and map display
- Use the Mileage Tracker for multiple businesses and multiple vehicles with a simple choice
- Setup frequent destinations and purposes for easy use later
- Choose either kilometers or miles
- Define custom rates for business, charity, medical and other
- Watch your deductions add up with each addition to your trip log
- Email HTML and Excel-friendly reports to your home computer
- Be used on or with iPhone/iPod Touch, Android OS, or WP8
- Make it easy to keep records for those who are always on the go
- Keep a central, simple place to track trip miles and expenses

Some other phone mileage tracker applications are:

- AutoMiles
- Klicks
- TaxMileage
- TripLog

When installing your mileage app into your phone, I would not use the free versions. The pay versions are extremely inexpensive. I think I only paid $2.99 for MileBug. It was a one-time fee. Make sure you spend a few bucks for the version of the app you choose to ensure that it works well.

Creating and Managing a budget

Setting up your working budget is going to be extremely important for your business. Once your working budget is established, you will be able to see how your actual spending compares with the budget. This will give you an idea of the health of your business as well as show you areas for change. Most business owners do not have a formal education in accounting. However, some of my business clients did take one or two accounting classes in college. This may not have fully prepared them for the sometimes-daunting task of accurate accounting and tax preparation. Just because you CAN doesn't always mean you SHOULD. I highly recommend having BlackBull or some other accounting firm set up your QuickBooks accounts. Your bookkeeping is going to roll right into your personal and business tax returns. If your accounts and books are not set up correctly, you stand to lose thousands of dollars in tax benefits and will not have an accurate picture of the health of your business.

Warning: Generally, bookkeepers and accountants do not have formal tax knowledge, training, certifications, and tax CPE (Continuing Professional Education). Similarly, tax professionals have not received formal accounting knowledge, training, and certifications. It is vitally important that your accountant specializes in BOTH accounting and tax preparation. You should not ask if your accountant can "do" both. Ask if they are certified, educated, and credentialed in both. Taxes and accounting are two completely different fields. Without competence in both fields, the bookkeeping and tax returns may be inconsistent, inaccurate, costly, and result in a full-blown audit.

Create expense accounts

Effective bookkeeping hinges on setting up your expense accounts correctly. Heck, all of your bookkeeping accounts need to be correct, but the "rubber meets the road" in the expense accounts. Your business might require 50-60 expense accounts. Most business owners can only think of 5 or 6. Expense accounts go way beyond rent, utilities, and insurance. At any time you should be able to produce accurate financial statements and see where all your revenue is coming from and where all of your money is being spent.

If you have a coffee station in your lobby, you should be able to find out exactly how much money you are spending on coffee, cream, and sugar with just a few clicks of your mouse. If you are unable to find this information, you are in the dark, baby. This is not where you want to be. This scenario will hold true for all of your business expenses. As a business owner, you need to be empowered. You need to know what is going on in your business. Wondering what is happening to your business is a horrible place to exist. You cannot effectively manage your business if you don't know what is going on. This starts with your chart of accounts. One reason BlackBull is so effective at our bookkeeping services is that not only do we have the formal education when it comes to accounting and taxes, but we have been small business owners for over 25 years.

Each tax season, I am still amazed to see how many new clients and their businesses have been managed incorrectly and inefficiently by other accountants, CPAs, MBAs, bookkeepers, and the business owners themselves. Being ignorant of effective tax laws and accounting principles may provide a false sense of relief to a business owner. If you don't know you are doing anything wrong, you don't worry about it. Ignorance is bliss in many cases. However, once BlackBull (or any other qualified firm) exposes the prior-year mistakes, things start to unravel quickly. Here are a couple of real-world examples:

Example 1 - This last tax season, I took on a new client. He has been running his small business for about 15 years now and is doing quite well. I set up his bookkeeping and completed his tax returns. As I started to compile his 2013 expenses, he was shocked at the number of questions I asked him. His prior

CPA asked him no such questions. I completed his books and tax returns. When comparing my figures to his prior-year taxes and financials, I discovered he was omitting approximately $15,000 in expenses. This equates to roughly $5,000 cash he should be receiving in tax savings. He was sickened to realize he was flushing $5,000 cash down the drain each year for the past seven years. His ignorance turned to disgust when he realized he has lost about $35,000 cash over that seven-year period. He asked me to start amending his prior-year tax returns.

Example 2 – Again, I took on a new client for the 2013 tax season, another small business owner that previously used a large, local, CPA firm. I showed him how we could convert over $3,000 in normally un-deductible expenses into deductible expenses. This new $3,000 deduction saved him over $900 in taxes which he normally pays to the IRS. This one tax-saving strategy more than paid for all of my bookkeeping. In essence, he received all of his bookkeeping for free and still ended up with cash in his pocket. Not too shabby.

Review on a regular basis

The marketplace is in constant flux. Businesses must change with market trends to stay competitive. It is important to review your business accounts and financials on a regular basis to make sure nothing is slipping through the cracks. Accounts in your chart of accounts might need to be made inactive, closed or added. Remember, how you think or feel your business is doing means nothing. What your books say your business is doing is what matters. Numbers don't lie. It will be wise for you to review your books at year-end (at a minimum) or quarterly (recommended) to stay on top of your business's health.

Set up your bookkeeping

If you purchase QuickBooks, you will see that is comes with the basic accounts set up for you. If you chose to use these generic settings without adding any custom accounts, your books will not be properly set up. Your financial statements will not adequately reflect the books and, consequently, will not efficiently translate to your tax returns. It's much easier to pay a professional to set up your books right from the start than it is fix them months or years down the road after you discover what a mess they are. The good news here is that money spent on a good accountant will come back to you ten-fold. If you try skimping to save a few hundred bucks on your bookkeeping set up, it could cost you thousands of dollars in the future.

When it comes to your bookkeeping, you have three options:

- **Do everything yourself** – You are responsible for the set-up, data entry, and management.

- **Pay a professional for your set-up** – You can pay to have your books set up correctly, but then you handle the data entry and management from there.

- **Pay a professional to manage your books for you** – You keep your hands clean and hire a professional to do your books for you. Your bookkeeper/accountant will set up your books and manage them monthly, quarterly, or provide a year-end "clean up." Even if you pay a professional, it should not give you an excuse to be ignorant of your financial position. Stay involved. Stay informed. Don't get lazy. That is how companies get ripped off for millions of dollars by their part-time bookkeeper. A bookkeeper in La Jolla, California, stole $3 million from Jack's Restaurant. You can read it here:

http://www.utsandiego.com/news/2014/aug/04/la-jolla-restaurant-bookkeeper-guilty-grand-theft/

The only two options I would recommend are 2 or 3. In fact, most business owners will contract out their bookkeeping even if the business owner is quite capable of doing their own books. Why? Bookkeeping is very stressful and time-consuming for someone who does not do it every day. It makes more sense for a business owner to pay a professional. This way, the business owner can focus on running the business and generating revenues. When I consult with my business owners, I often use the following analogy:

The Oil Change

Can I change the oil in my car by myself? Yes, I am very capable.
Do I change my own oil? Heck no.

The last time I changed my own car oil was back in 1990. Why? Changing my own oil stopped penciling out for me as a good use of resources. Why would I spend three hours of my time, make a mess on my garage floor, generate a jug of oil and filter I need to dump, lose time with my business or family, and still have to pay for my new oil and filter when I can use a coupon and have my oil changed for $30? By hiring a professional I don't get dirty, I don't have to get rid of a filter and jug of oil, I save 2 ½ hours, and I can get caught up on my phone calls while eating a sandwich.

When starting your new business, there are plenty of things on which you will be able to skimp, and should. I don't believe your bookkeeping should be one of them.

Organize your source documents

It is important to keep organized records of your source documents in the event you receive a request for more information from the IRS. Make sure your office printer is able to scan as well. Source documents include:

- Checklists
- Microfiches
- Mileage logs
- Credit memos
- Time sheets
- Deposit slips
- Charts
- Notes
- Receipts
- Invoices
- Negatives
- Travel itineraries
- Credit card statements
- Bank statements
- Automated files
- Magnetic media
- Cash register tapes
- Canceled checks

Source docs validate the tax return if the IRS, or state agency, has any questions. This is why establishing a business bank account and business credit card is so beneficial. Monthly and year-end statements list your business transactions and can be imported into accounting software. You will want to keep your source docs organized and safe. If you really want to be a super star, you can scan all of your source docs (when in paper format) and save to a .pdf file on your hard drive. Having digital versions of your source docs can be extremely helpful. Your files can be easily stored, organized, transported, shared, and kept safe. At BlackBull we do everything we can to keep our source docs digital.

Chapter 9

Efficiencies and Best Practices

Take my word for it, the last thing you want to do is continue to re-invent the wheel. When running your business, you will not want to perpetually be "winging it" or figuring things out as you go. The goal with your business operations will be to identify your "sweet spot." The sweet spot is where you are at maximum efficiency. If you really want to master the efficiencies in your business, you should learn more about the Six Sigma concept. You can do a Google search on "Six Sigma" or go to http://office.microsoft.com/en-us/visio-help/improve-your-process-and-your-bottom-line-with-six-sigma-HA001123336.aspx?CTT=5&origin=HA001165913 to learn more. Be smart. Be efficient.

The way to find your sweet spot is to take notes at the end of each day. Document the procedures and actions which worked well for you and those which did not. Repeat the effective actions; eliminate the ineffective ones. Keep a log of daily activity and then analyze weekly. This process weeds out inefficiency and promotes efficiency. Pretty soon, you will be able to create your operations manual based on your "best practices." Best practices will be part of your Six Sigma business strategy. When best practices work within an efficient business, expenses and labor can be reduced while revenues and profits climb.

Six Sigma

Six Sigma is a powerful approach to improving processes to do things better, faster, and at lower cost to virtually eliminate defects. It can be applied to every facet of business, from production, to human resources, to order entry, to technical support. Six Sigma started in the mid-1980s at Motorola in response to the needs of a sales force faced with increasing customer dissatisfaction and competitive pressures. To address these problems, Motorola created a set of formulas and tools that identified and measured what was important to their customers and then applied the findings to performance. Toyota is also seen as a Six Sigma pioneer.

Any activity concerned with cost, timeliness, and quality of results can benefit from the Six Sigma approach. Unlike other quality improvement efforts, Six Sigma uses a specific philosophy, measure, and methodology to provide tangible savings that are directly traceable to the bottom line. The benefits of Six Sigma include:

- A clear focus on activities and attributes that are absolutely crucial to customers
- The elimination of process variation and inconsistency
- Targeted improvements that provide the largest financial return on investment and can be measured by increased profit, revenue, and customer satisfaction
- Far-reaching shifts in company behavior and the active participation of top management

The Six Sigma Philosophy

The Six Sigma philosophy addresses the following:

- What is serious to your customers?

- How well are you performing today?
- How can you leverage facts and data?
- How can you sustain improvement?

Six Sigma encourages you and your organization to focus on what is absolutely critical to your customer by:

- Improving quality and performance in the areas of greatest reward
- Translating what is critical to customers into something measurable

Ultimately, reward is measured by increased profitability and increased customer satisfaction. To effectively improve the performance of your business, you must be able to measure quantitatively what your customers consider essential about your products or services. Six Sigma converts qualitative attributes into a metric. Facts and data are the backbone of Six Sigma. They are equally as important as a thorough understanding of customers' CTQs (critical to quality), because they are the basis for the decisions you make and the actions you take to improve your process. When you leverage facts and data, you:

- Remove personal reactions and preferences as stumbling blocks
- Eliminate both trial and error and gut feel as problem-solving tools
- Encourage more efficient problem solving by identifying the best solution early
- Validate the actions leading to improvement

The Six Sigma efficiency goal is 99.99966% efficiency. Don't freak out. Let me explain. The difference between 99.99966% efficiency and 99% efficiency can be thought of as the "hidden office." The hidden office represents all activity that results in defects (not meeting customer expectations) or not doing things right following the first attempt. Customers don't pay for the hidden office, you do!

For example, say a company bills eight million customers on a monthly basis. If the process were performing at a 99% success rate, 80,000 customers would be incorrectly billed each month. The hidden office represents the costs and resources required to find and fix incorrect billings, and to address customer dissatisfaction. With a 99.99966% efficiency, there would only be 27 customers billed incorrectly. Imagine the resources saved if 79,973 bills don't have to be corrected? Because Six Sigma targets improvements for financial gain, it's crucial to understand how much it costs a business to run at less than Six Sigma capability. What is the cost associated with not meeting customer expectations or with not doing things right at the first attempt?

Let's take a look at BlackBull. What if I prepared 600 tax returns with a 99% success rate? That would mean that 594 returns were successfully filed. That would also mean I would need to deal with six problematic tax returns. The time required to fix or amend those six returns could cost me 10 – 20 hours depending on the issues. This includes the time I would spend on the phone with the customers, the IRS, and state agencies. And what if there were penalties and interest? Looking at it this way, a 99% success rate does not seem very attractive. The goal of Six Sigma does.

Best Practices

As your business grows, you will need to change to adapt to new circumstances. You can experiment with different ways of working to see which suits your business best. This approach can be inefficient at first and may lead you to make inappropriate decisions. Remember, don't forget to take notes as you go. Once you see the negative impacts, change your behavior to create positive impacts. I suggest logging results in a spreadsheet and tracking them like a hound.

Track phone calls made, messages left, people reached, appointments booked, and track what factors might affect these statistics. The day, time, seasons, sports, holidays, weather, and the like can impact your results. Identify your variable factors and determine where the best practice is located. Do this also with quotes, estimates, designs, colors, projects, marketing campaigns, etc. Don't just trust how you think or feel things are going. Take notes and let the facts speak for themselves. We learned that our company's FaceBook page received virtually no response when posts were made during the week; however, posting in the evening on a Friday got the highest response. Why? After thinking about it, I deduced that the BlackBull posts were lost in a sea of activity during the work week. When everyone shut it down for the weekend, they actually took time to read FaceBook and took notice of what we were posting. I have been through this with a few of my companies. There were things we felt one way about, but learned were not true by tracking results.

You are smart enough to know that you do not need to re-invent the wheel. In your quest for best practices, see how successful businesses operate and introduce their ways of working into your business. Reduce your learning curve. Save time, money, and headaches. You are reading this book, aren't you? Good job. A best practice strategy can help your business to:

- Become more competitive
- Increase sales and develop new markets
- Reduce costs and become more efficient

- Improve the skills of your workforce
- Use technology more effectively
- Reduce waste and improve quality
- Respond more quickly to innovations in your sector

How to find your Best Practice "Sweet Spot"

Best Practice means finding and using the best ways of working efficiently and effectively to achieve your business goals. It involves keeping up to date with the ways that successful businesses operate in your field and measuring your ways of working against those used by the market leaders around you.

Best Practice - Benchmarking
Applying Best Practice means learning from and through the experience of others. Simply put, copy your competitors. One way of doing this is through benchmarking. Benchmarking allows you to compare your business with other successful businesses to highlight areas where your business could improve. But don't stop there. Sometimes you will compare your business to itself and the benchmarks you create.

Best Practice - Standards
Standards are fixed specifications or benchmarks, which are established by independent or government bodies. There are both technical and management standards. Technical standards are precise specifications against which a business can measure the quality of its product, service or processes. Management standards (below) are models for achieving best business and organizational practice. Applying the appropriate standards to your business will enable you to apply best practices and work against

objective criteria to achieve manufacturing or service quality. It's a mouthful, but it works.

Best Practice - Management

Management best practice involves:
- The communication of a clear mission and strategy
- Leadership by example and mentoring
- The setting of demanding but realistic targets
- An open and communicative management style
- Clear and careful strategic planning

There are several business tools that you can use to achieve management best practice, including:
- Benchmarking
- Forecasting
- Financial planning
- Strategic planning
- Performance monitoring

A very effective way of monitoring your business is to introduce key performance indicators (KPIs). These can be used to measure progress in achieving business objectives across a range of activities and enable you to identify areas that need attention. KPIs can be used to measure activities such as sales volumes, profitability, quality, and staff turnover. The indicators you choose will depend on your specific business. They should, however, be related to your overall objectives, be clearly measurable, and provide an indication of where improvements need to be made.

Tools such as benchmarking, business planning, and performance monitoring will help you to compare the performance of your business with that of your peers and competitors and against your own business objectives. Where necessary, you can introduce new ways of working to improve competitiveness and business efficiency. Having accurate and up-to-date information about your business performance will also help future planning and change management. Communicating your objectives and strategies is an essential part of management best practice. A good communications policy will ensure that everyone in your business knows the direction in which the business is heading, and understands their own part in its development. Employee suggestion box, anyone?

Best Practice - Employees

Successful businesses are those that attract, develop, motivate, and retain the best people. You will get the most benefit from your staff if you have key strategies for doing so. These can include:

- Involving employees in the development of the business
- Communicating with employees with an Open-Door policy
- Flexible work policies and policies that encourage equality and diversity
- Setting targets and rewarding achievement
- Offering employee development and training
- Providing fringe benefits and a rewards program

Employees are often in a position to see where improvements can be made or when market demands are changing. Your staff might be aware of inefficient production processes, while customer service staff will know common sources of complaints. You can use this detailed knowledge by involving employees in developing improved ways of working. This is likely to make your staff feel valued, as well as gaining employee trust, commitment, and buy-in when implementing changes. This is also a great time to document the areas that might need improvement. Involve the employee by asking them to establish a criterion for testing and tracking the results. Then they can compile the results to "prove" their case for a suggested change.

Good people management should extend across all areas of your business. Recruitment, training, working practices, and the working environment are all areas which you should continually review to see where improvements can be made. People management systems such as performance appraisals, quality circles, cascade briefings, 360 degree feedback, and internal communications will help you to get the best from your employees.

Best Practice – Operations
Most businesses have some operational issues that can be improved through the introduction of best practice methods, including:

- Quality management
- Stock control, delivery, and supply chain management
- Purchasing and ordering
- Information management

You can identify which operational areas will benefit from best practice methods by:
- Benchmarking
- Internal analysis

- Reviewing appropriate national and international standards

Areas for improvement could include the introduction of quality management systems such as Total Quality Management, automated stock control, just-in-time ordering and delivery, and "lean" manufacturing and supply. When you have identified the areas for improvement, you can implement changes. It is important, however, to keep your employees, suppliers and customers aware of what you are doing, and to make sure that the changes do not cause unnecessary disruption to your business.

Best Practice - Sales and Marketing
Sales are huge. The right sales and marketing strategies will play an essential role in the success of your business. Developments in technology have opened up entirely new ways to market and sell products and services. Best practice now involves harnessing the power of the Internet, email, and mobile telephony to increase the effectiveness of getting products and services to the customer. As you know, even the smallest business can benefit from having a website. Many organizations also use electronic newsletters (also known as e-zines), regular emails, and SMS (text) messaging to communicate with their markets. There are some good websites to help you with your texting and text blasts. You can look at:

- CallFire.com
- EZTexting.com
- TextSendr.com
- Twilio.com
- Pinger.com
- TextingHome.com
- Textem.com
- TextNow.com
- Joopz.com

I have used Joopz extensively. It works amazingly well. Web-based texting offers two-way web texting, group messaging, scheduled messages, affordability, flexibility, and security. All sizes of companies use this type of web-based technology. My doctor sends me text message appointment reminders, RedBox sends me coupons and reminders for movie releases, and

Southwest Airlines sends me flight status updates via text message. The benefits of alternative e-marketing include:

- Broad reach - a website, email, or text can reach visitors from all over
- Lower costs - a website, emails, and texts are more cost effective than using traditional stores, marketing, and postage
- Level playing field - small businesses can compete alongside the websites of much larger businesses
- Better targeting – emails and texts are less likely to be opened by someone else, and opt-in mailing lists ensure that your message is read by someone who wants to receive it
- New markets – e-Marketing makes it easier to target customers who were previously out of reach

As with all best practice, it is important to get the implementation right. Your website needs to be crafted carefully and updated regularly.

Warning: You need to be aware of possible legislation that applies to electronic business communications, including selling from websites.

Best Practice - Innovation
Fostering a culture of innovation and creativity in your business can help you stay one step ahead of your competitors by ensuring that your products and services remain up to date and in line with what your customers need. You will be able to react more quickly to changing markets, customer expectations and needs, and you are likely to see changes coming before others do. Best practice in innovation involves constantly looking at your existing products, processes, and procedures to see what improvements can be made to keep them at the cutting edge. This is also part of your efficiency

protocol.

Innovative businesses often have strong, inspirational leaders and management, and well-trained and motivated employees. These businesses maintain a culture of innovation, constantly looking at every aspect of the organization, not just its products, pricing, and services. They ask the question, "How can things be done better?"

Innovation may come in the form of small changes to existing products or services or in the form of a completely new product or service. The innovation may come from internal sources such as a product development team or be inspired by external forces such as customer requests or developments in related technologies. Have a company suggestion box and make sure your website has a feature allowing customers to contact you or leave feedback. At BlackBull our clients have contributed much to the way we run our business. Many features on our website and even the title of this book were based on our clients' contributions.

Best Practice – Information Technology (IT)
It is possible to give your business a distinct competitive advantage by making good use of IT. High-speed telephone networks, along with the Internet, enable you to communicate even more effectively and to distribute information quickly and accurately (Note: I review my internet/data plan with my carrier every year to get the best service at the best price). The Internet has revolutionized the way businesses communicate with customers and suppliers in marketing, information access, and product distribution. In larger organizations, intranets and extranets, internal and external communications networks, are used to communicate with employees, customers, suppliers and other stakeholders. High-speed Internet access is fast and allows everyone in an organization to be online all the time. This improves business efficiency and, because it is available for a

fixed monthly charge, it is easier to control costs.

Along with wireless networking and mobile communication, the Internet enables new ways of deploying staff. "Hot-desking," "telecommuting," and "virtual teams" allow increased productivity, improved communication, and more flexible working methods. Even in the smallest companies, integrated databases and systems can bring significant cost savings and improvements in efficiency. And who doesn't want some of that?

Warning: IT security is a serious issue. Mobile telephony and wireless networking increases the chance of security breaches. It is important to adopt best practice for IT security. Ensure you have appropriate controls to safeguard information access, passwords, firewalls, and security software. Make sure all of your employees are fully-trained in their use.

To learn more about Best Practices, go to:
http://www.infoentrepreneurs.org/en/guides/best-practice/

Making Changes

How are you when it comes to making changes in life? Do you resist change or embrace it? If you are fearful of change, I'm afraid small business ownership might not be for you. In case you have not noticed, finding best practices is all about change. Some changes are subtle; some are monumental. The business world is all about change. After I completed the section of this book about best practices, I assumed I made my point about the importance of change. Fortunately, I have learned to pause and be cautious when making assumptions. After some consideration, I felt it necessary to be deliberate and make a clear point about the intimate relationship between change, business, and the business owner.

As you know, I am fascinated by economics. During my studies, I stumbled upon a quote from the Irish playwright and co-founder of the London School of Economics, George Bernard Shaw. Shaw famously said, **"Progress is impossible without change, and those who cannot <u>change their minds</u> cannot change anything."** This quote has stuck with me over the years, and now is the perfect time to share it with you. I am using Shaw to make my point. Unless you are capable of change, I believe your business will not reach its potential or will fail altogether. I underlined a key point in Shaw's quote. Change must include the ability to not only change your behavior, but more importantly, also <u>change your mind</u>.

What is the difference between changing your behavior and changing your mind? Why is this distinction so important? The ability to change your mind shows the ability to overcome emotional attachments. Simply changing a behavior, in my opinion, will not ensure the potential for long-term success. This point goes back to the philosophy of being a business owner. The actions of a business owner need to be in unity with the business owners philosophy, not in conflict with them. Ok, enough of the riddles. Let me explain myself by sharing another quick story.

An Italian restaurant owner of 35 years was watching her restaurant slowly decline over an eight year period. She blamed it on a poor economy, the rising cost of food, and competition. She was not blaming herself or her staff. After eight years of declining sales, she found herself in over $400,000 of debt and was losing her house, her restaurant, and her family. As a last resort, she hired a consultant to analyze her restaurant operations in an attempt to find and fix the problems. To the consultant, the problems were as obvious as the empty seats in her restaurant. She was providing horrible food, horrible service, and horrible staff management. She was 100% of the problem. When the issues were pointed out to her, her response was not one of gratitude, but one of denial. After 27 years of success, she could not believe that the last eight years were her fault. She was emotionally attached to the restaurant, her staff, and her errant business operations. She developed a false sense of security based on false assumptions. To further make my point, let me tell you about the "sauce."

This restaurant owner was using a marinara sauce which has been a family recipe for nearly 300 years. She believed the sauce was the cornerstone of her restaurant and her family's legacy. How do you think she reacted when the restaurant consultant told her that her sauce was terrible? If she wanted her restaurant to survive, it was essential that she come up with a new and improved marinara sauce recipe. The consultant, who was also a master chef, helped her create a new recipe for a much-improved and fresh marinara sauce. The problem of the sub-standard sauce was now solved, right? Well, not exactly. This is where the behavior change versus mind change is so important.

The restaurant owner had an emotional attachment to a 300 year old family sauce recipe of Biblical proportions. If she only changed her behavior, she would have served the new sauce for a short period of time until her irrational and emotional attachment would have justified bring the old sauce back. It was only after a blind taste test when she understood how much better the new sauce was. As a result, she was able to change her <u>mind</u> first, then change her <u>behavior,</u> and serve the new sauce with trust and conviction. She changed her mind and behavior about most of her business operations and was able to turn her restaurant around. Again, changing your mind and behavior is not always easy, but it is essential for your business to survive and thrive. Remember, what once was may no longer be. What worked yesterday may not work tomorrow. This is the nature of business.

Client Contracts, Agreements, and Letters of Engagement

I wish I had a dollar for every time one of my past clients said, "Wow, this feels like I'm buying a home," when the paperwork portion of our transaction took place. My background is vast and includes intellectual property, real estate, mortgages, home remodeling, print advertising, and television. In every transaction, there was a pile of paper to sign. Contracts, agreements, and engagement letters are part of doing business. Get used to it. Even if your customers don't need to sign anything, as the business owner, you certainly will. If you have "clients," most likely they will be signing your documents to do business with you. These documents are very important. They do away with the handshake deal and put everything on paper to protect both parties. Contracts usually include these elements to address:

- An offer and acceptance
- Intention to be legally bound
- Consideration
- Performance
- Terms
- Limits to contract
- Remedies for breach

Policies, Terms of Use, Disclosures, and Disclaimers

These are the details. Such documents could be required by your industry, state guidelines, or federal guidelines. You may need to provide copies of your policies, terms, disclosures, and disclaimers to your clients. They may need to sign for them as well. Your disclosures may be in addition to your contracts and agreements or might be stand-alone. Such documents could be vital to the health of your company. If your industry does not require them, as a business owner, you should consider them anyway. These forms protect you and your clients and keep you compliant. Do not try to sidestep them. In the past, I would apologize for the inconvenience they caused. I don't do that anymore. I fully embrace them and educate my clients if necessary. Disclosures can outline:

- What your business will do
- What your business does not do
- Client requirements
- Dispute Resolution
- Levels of uncertainty
- Eligibility requirements
- Signatures and approvals
- Mediation and Arbitration
- Scope of services
- Scope of rights
- Fee structure
- Warranties
- Liabilities
- Timelines
- Obligations
- Waivers
- Risks
- Damages
- Penalties
- Rules
- Duty of care
- Privacy

Contracts, disclosures, and the like will generate paperwork. Your paperwork will need to be managed effectively.

Fine print

Speaking of disclosures, this reminds me of something. Does your business involve paperwork with fine print? You know, those pesky disclosures you are not too happy about? Be aware of fine print, both your fine print and the fine print of others with whom you do business. I have always tried to eliminate any fine print when operating my businesses. I put my disclosures in full-size print and do not shy away from them. I have found that businesses or professionals who use or hide behind fine print immediately lose credibility and goodwill. This creates distrust. The business owners who are proud of their disclosure practices gain the trust of their clients much quicker and easier. In fact, your best customers and clients will expect you to have disclosures as part of running a successful business practice. Not having such policies and disclosures actually undermines your business. Embrace them; do not ever apologize or shy away from them. Disclose what you need to and make sure you use your "grown-up" font.

Two wrongs don't make a right

As a business owner, you will be wronged and taken advantage of at some point. You will have clients who do not pay their bills; you will have clients or customers file law suits against you; you will have employees who steal from you; or you might have others slander your good name. This sucks. It feels horrible when it happens. You might beat yourself up trying to figure out why it is happening. I can tell you, that is a rabbit hole with no bottom. I have found three very effective strategies for dealing with such situations:

1) Be amazing. Be your best. Offer great service, treat others right, and do not cut corners. Remain humble and keep a great attitude. Doing these things can eliminate most of your problems. If not, try the next two.

2) Be insured. Having the correct insurance policies in place can remove most of your worry.

3) Be willing to concede. A worker's compensation processor once told me, *"Sometimes in proving you are right, you can become wrong."* The point here is to make sure you keep your head when others lose theirs.

Don't lose yourself in the chaos. It's not worth it. Focus on the amazing clients and customers you have and try not to dwell on the few bad ones. This can be difficult. No one likes to be falsely accused of anything or unjustly treated. Prepare to have your character challenged when these situations come up but don't become a monster.

File Maintenance and Security

Good record keeping is going to be essential for your business. If you are not feeling well, you might go to a doctor. During your office visit, your doctor will ask you a series of questions to diagnose your condition. The same holds true for your business. If your business is not feeling well, it will tell you what's wrong through the financial statements and records. Maintaining good records can benefit you and your company in a number of ways. Keeping good records:

- Helps to maximize all the expenses you claim
- Reduces your tax obligations
- Will help out during inquiries and investigations
- Makes it quicker to prepare your accounts at year-end
- Gives you the information you need to run your business and help it grow
- Helps you plan for tax payments
- Helps identify the strengths and weaknesses in your business
- Helps manage changes and improvements in your business
- Helps plan for financial commitments
- Makes it easier to get a loan or sell your business

- Avoids over/under tax payments
- Helps identify if your business is liable for paying special taxes
- Makes it easier to distribute profits and dividends to shareholders
- Streamlines partnership distributions where both profits and losses have to be shared

Do you hate paperwork? Join the club. You are not alone. Rather than practicing your eye rolling and heavy breathing, you need to embrace the paperwork portion of your business and come up with an effective management system. You don't need to over-complicate the process. Keep it simple and use effective tools to help you. Here are a few tips that might help:

Set up appropriate filing baskets – You can dump, I mean neatly stack, your paperwork in organized document baskets. Block "paperwork" time in your schedule. When things are less stressful, you can put on some music and process your paperwork stacks. Make the process as fun as possible. Have some snacks and a drink. This will help change your perspective on filing and paperwork.

Create digital files – I encourage you to scan your original documents to create digital files. At BlackBull, we scan all documents and create .pdf formats if we don't have copies in Word or Adobe already. This way, you will have a paper copy and a digital copy. Redundancy is a good idea in record keeping.

I also recommend downloading a .pdf writer (printer) if your computer does not have one. This way you can convert all docs in a non-.pdf format to pdf. If your computer does not have Adobe or the ability to "save as" a .pdf document, this printer will install just like your desktop printer. It works wonderfully. Go to www.cutepdf.com to download it. You can install a converter or a writer (printer).

Storage - There are different storage methods you can use.

On-site storage - This can include paper files in file cabinets and digital files stored on your computer or external hard drive.

Off-site storage - This can include physical storage in file cabinets and file boxes stored in a safe, dry, fireproof, secure storage facility. This also includes cloud storage on an off-site server. Here is a cloud storage Top-17 list I created:

- JustCloud.com
- ZipCloud.com
- LiveDrive.com
- Carbonite.com
- BackBlaze.com
- CrashPlan.com
- Zoolz.com
- Mozy.com
- Mega.co.nz
- 4Shared.com
- DropBox.com
- OneDrive.com
- SOSOnlineBackup.com
- Google.com (Google Drive)
- SafeCopyBackup.com
- SugarSync.com
- SpiderOak.com

You can see the side-by-side comparison of these companies at: http://www.bestcloudstorage.net/

Cloud storage has been around for years, but it has really become an essential tool as of late. Cloud storage is a model of data storage where the digital data is stored in logical pools, the physical storage spans across multiple servers (and often locations), and the physical environment is typically owned and managed by a hosting company. These cloud storage providers are responsible for keeping the data available and accessible, and the physical environment protected and running. People and organizations buy or lease storage capacity from the providers to store end user, organization, or application data. If you are new to the cloud storage game, here are 10 reasons why it might make sense for you:

1. **Cost** – Backing up your data isn't always cheap, especially when you factor in the cost of any equipment needed to do so (external hard drives or backup tapes). Additionally, there is the cost of the time it takes to manually complete routine backups. Online storage services reduce much of the cost associated with traditional backup methods, providing ample storage space in the cloud for a low monthly fee.

2. **Invisibility** – For all intents and purposes, cloud storage is invisible; with no physical presence. It doesn't take up valuable space at home or in the office. There is no foot print.

3. **Security** – Storing confidential or sensitive information in the cloud is often more secure than storing it locally, especially for businesses. With online storage services, data is encrypted both during transmission and while at rest, ensuring no unauthorized users can access the files. Local storage can be damaged or stolen. Children and sippy cups don't mix well with computers and hard drives.

4. **Automation** – The biggest issue most consumers and businesses have with backing up is follow-through; it simply just doesn't get done. Online storage services make the tedious process of backing up easy to accomplish through automation. You simply select what and when you want to back up, and the service does the rest.

5. **Accessibility** – From tablets to smartphones, netbooks to desktops, we're using more devices on a daily basis than ever before, and toggling files between each of these devices can be cumbersome and complex. Not so with online storage services. You can access your account from

any internet connection, whether you're on a mobile browser or your work computer.

6. **Syncing** – Syncing ensures your files are automatically updated across all of your devices. This way, the latest version of a file you saved on your desktop is available on your smartphone.

7. **Sharing** – Whether you want to share a single photo or an entire folder with hundreds of documents, online storage services allow you to easily share files with just a few clicks.

8. **Collaboration** – Online storage services are also ideal for collaboration purposes. They allow multiple people to edit and collaborate on a single file or document. You don't have to worry about tracking the latest version or who has made what changes. This is a big deal in my world.

9. **Protection** – Cloud storage serves as an added layer of data protection for your precious and irreplaceable files. Backups are kept in a secure location that is physically removed from the originals.

10. **Recovery** – In the event of catastrophic data loss, you'll have backups of all your original files so you can restore them with zero downtime.

CONCLUSION

In this book, I have managed to condense weeks of one-on-one small-business consulting into just over 200 pages. I wanted not only to address the "How-To" Step-by-Step, process (including checklists) of building a business, but also the philosophy behind the "Why Should or Shouldn't I" start a small business.

I have attempted to provide a content-rich format that allows you to learn at your own pace. Some chapters are easily understandable while others are heavy in content and might introduce you to some new concepts and philosophy. You are not required to take notes or even remember the things I am trying to teach you. It is all laid out before you in a convenient reference tool which is designed to make your life easier and assist with the health of your new business. The Small Business Start-Up Workbook is designed to provide you with a roadmap to starting your business, save you thousands of dollars in consulting fees, and keep you from making mistakes. Mistakes in business can be quite costly. Mistakes lead to "now-I-know" moments. You will want to avoid or limit these "learning opportunities" as much as possible. Over the years, I have accumulated hundreds of thousands of dollars in "now-I-know" moments. They stink!

Business is a living, breathing organism. Your business and the business environment will be ever-changing. I know I will need to amend this book and issue later editions to conform to market changes. I would appreciate your help in this process. If you feel you have anything to add to this book to improve it, please let me know. Call or email me. I will be happy to entertain your input and comments and have no problem incorporating them into future edition releases.

Thank you for taking the time to read The Small Business Start-Up Workbook. I hope it was helpful to you, your business, and your family. If you would like any one-on-one consulting to follow up this book, please let me know.

All the best,

Mark A. Torr
Owner – BlackBull Accounting, Inc.
mark@blackbullaccounting.com

DISCLAIMER

The Small Business Start-Up Workbook content is for your general information and use only. We do not guarantee the accuracy of its content and assume no liability for any inaccuracies. Use of information is at your own risk. This book contains copyright material owned by us and other entities; reproduction is prohibited. All websites in this workbook are the property of their respective owners. Web links to other websites are provided for your convenience. We do not endorse or have responsibility for the content of other websites. Any rights not expressly granted herein are reserved.

Mark A. Torr

APPENDICES

Appendix A – Employee vs. Business Owner

(Please complete surveys and questions with pencil. You may amend your answers from time to time)

	Employee		Business Owner	
	Yes	No	Yes	No
Convenient work hours				
Commuting / Traffic issues				
High cost of fuel or transportation				
High cost of wardrobe or uniforms				
Provides appropriate levels of income				
Provides structured lunches or breaks				
Overtime pay availability				
Paid holidays				
Paid sick days				
Insurance benefits				
High levels of stress and responsibility				
Professional support / back office available				
Obligation to clients				
Workplace, furniture, and tools				
Provides education and training				
Maximizes your skillset				
Room to achieving your potential				
Power to make decisions				
Politics in the workplace				
Demands time away from family				

	Employee		Business Owner	
	Yes	No	Yes	No
Conforms with 5, 10, 20 year plan				
Addresses retirement considerations				
Conforms with desired lifestyle				
Builds own self-worth				

Appendix B – Deciding on a Business

1. What are you good (proficient) at? _____
   _____
   _____

2. Do you currently have a hobby you are passionate about? _____
   If so, what? _____
   _____

3. What do you enjoy doing? _____
   _____
   _____

4. What inspires you? _____
   _____
   _____

5. Which occupation will hold your attention? _____
   _____
   _____

6. Which option provides the best income opportunity? _____
   _____
   _____

7. Which option provides the best longevity? _____
   _____
   _____

8. What are the physical demands (wear and tear on your body)? _____
_____
_____

9. Would you rather use your mind or your back to get your job done?___
_____
_____

10. Are you able to handle and enjoy repetition?_____
_____
_____

11. Are you able to handle rejection and negative criticism?_____
_____
_____

12. Which option is best for your family?_____
_____
_____

13. Which option provides the most flexibility?_____
_____
_____

14. Which option has the smallest barrier to entry? _____
_____
_____

15. What do the start-up costs look like for each option? _____
_____
_____

16. What are the education, certification, licensing, and credential requirements?_____
_____
_____

17. Which option will rejuvenate you? _____
_____
_____

18. Which option will deplete you? _____
_____
_____

19. Do you prefer to work with others or work alone?_____
_____
_____

20. Would you like to hire a staff to help run things or operate by yourself?
_____
_____
_____

21. Would you rather speak or listen? _____
_____
_____

22. Would you prefer a retail store front or a retail website? _____
_____
_____

23. Would you rather market yourself by word of mouth or by running an ad? _____
_____

24. Would you like to have your name on a store front or remain anonymous? _____
_____

25. Do you prefer to have a large client list or relatively small one? _____
_____

26. Do you desire to have passive income down the road? _____
_____

27. Do you intend to sell your business one day? _____
_____

28. Do you plan to hand your business down to someone else? _____
_____

29. Which option will be impacted by business cycles or seasonal weather?
_____
_____

30. Do you prefer moderate steady income or larger income with volatility?
_____
_____

31. Do you prefer to work indoors or out? _____
_____

32. Do you prefer physical labor and activity or prefer working from an office chair? _____
_____

33. Do you prefer to travel, work on the road, or stay put? _____
_____
_____

34. Will your business be able to relocate if you decide to move? _____
_____
_____

35. Would you prefer to help existing clients or find new ones? _____
_____

36. Do you prefer an existing business or would like to create a new company from scratch? _____
_____
_____

37. Would you rather talk to someone about something or actually do something? _____
_____

38. Do you prefer a home-based office, commercial space, or store front?
_____
_____

39. Do you like to have structure or figure things out as you go? _____
_____
_____

40. Do you enjoy negotiations or do you prefer to have things fixed? _____
_____
_____

41. Would you rather see your clients happy or see a good income? _____
_____

42. Would you rather invest money or time into your new business? _____
_____

43. Do you prefer to be creative or administrative? _____
_____

44. Would you rather work with machines or people? _____
_____

45. How do you feel about adopting technology? _____
_____
_____

46. How do you feel about paperwork, reports, organization, and storage?
_____
_____
_____

47. Would you prefer to explain your business to a person or group of people? _____
_____

Appendix C – Business Survey

1. What do you like most about our new product (service)?

2. What changes would most improve our new product (service)?

3. What do you like most about competing products (services) currently available from other companies?

4. What changes would most improve competing products (services) currently available from other companies?

5. What would make you more likely to use our new product (service)?

6. If our new product (service) were available today, how likely would you be to recommend it to others?
   - ☐ Extremely likely
   - ☐ Very likely
   - ☐ Moderately likely
   - ☐ Slightly likely
   - ☐ Not likely at all

7. If you are not likely to use our new product (service), why not?
   - ☐ Do not need a product (service) like this
   - ☐ Do not want a product (service) like this
   - ☐ Satisfied with competing products (services) currently available
   - ☐ Cannot pay for a product (service) like this
   - ☐ Not willing to pay for a product (service) like this
   - ☐ Other (please specify):

8. How important is price to you when choosing this type of company?
   - ☐ Extremely important
   - ☐ Quite important
   - ☐ Moderately important
   - ☐ Slightly important
   - ☐ Not at all important

9. Overall, how satisfied are you with your experience using our new product (service)?
   - ☐ Extremely satisfied
   - ☐ Quite satisfied
   - ☐ Somewhat satisfied
   - ☐ Neither satisfied nor dissatisfied
   - ☐ Somewhat dissatisfied
   - ☐ Quite dissatisfied
   - ☐ Extremely dissatisfied

10. If our new product (service) were available today, how likely would you be to use it instead of competing products currently available from other companies?
    - ☐ Extremely likely
    - ☐ Very likely
    - ☐ Moderately likely
    - ☐ Slightly likely
    - ☐ Not likely at all

11. If our new company were available today, how likely would you be to recommend it to others?
    - ☐ Extremely likely
    - ☐ Very likely
    - ☐ Moderately likely
    - ☐ Slightly likely
    - ☐ Not likely at all

12. How important is convenience when choosing this type of product (service)?
    - ☐ Extremely important
    - ☐ Quite important
    - ☐ Moderately important
    - ☐ Slightly important
    - ☐ Not at all important

Appendix D – Simple Business Plans

Example A

Overview
- What will you sell?
- Who will buy it?
- How will your business help people?

Revenues
- What will you charge?
- How will you get paid?
- What are all the sources of revenue for your business?

Marketing
- How will others learn about your business?
- How will you encourage referrals?

Success Goals
- How many customers do you need?
- What annual revenues do you need?
- What is your timeline to reach these goals?

Challenges
- What are your challenges?
- What are your solutions?

Example B

Vision - What are you creating?

Mission - Why are you creating your business?

Objectives - What will you measure?
(examples)
- Revenue
- Profits
- Number of clients
- Sales
- Growth
- Number of employees
- Markets

Strategies – What will make your business successful over time?
(Examples)
- Becoming an industry expert
- Exposure and the media
- Publishing
- Coaching
- Creating programs
- Endorsements
- Exit strategy
- Collaboration

Action Plans – What work needs to be done?
(Examples)
- Publicity and marketing plan
- Growth plan

- Site plan
- Financial plan
- Budget plan

Appendix E – SWOT Analysis

Internal Analysis – Strengths and Weaknesses
External Analysis – Opportunities and Threats

Strengths
A firm's strengths are its resources and capabilities that can be used as a basis for developing a competitive advantage. Examples of such strengths include:
- Patents
- Strong brand names and company name
- Good reputation among customers
- Cost advantages from proprietary know-how
- Exclusive access to resources
- Favorable access to distribution networks
- Human resources of the owner and staff
- Industry knowledge
- Certified skills
- Flexibility

Weaknesses
The absence of certain strengths may be viewed as a weakness. For example, each of the following may be considered a weakness:
- Lack of patent protection
- A weak brand name or company name
- Poor reputation among customers
- High cost structure
- Lack of access to resources
- Lack of access to key distribution channels
- Liability exposure

In some cases, a weakness may be the flip side of a strength. Take the case in which a company has a large amount of manufacturing capacity. While this capacity may be considered a strength that competitors do not share, it also may be a considered a weakness if the large investment in manufacturing capacity prevents the firm from reacting quickly to changes in the strategic environment. Weaknesses may also be the platform for opportunities. For example, a weakness might be a smaller than needed shop space. That could lead to an opportunity for expansion. Another weakness might be sole proprietorship because the company is most likely personality driven with liability an issue.

Opportunities
Internal and external environmental analysis may reveal certain new opportunities for profit and growth. Some examples of such opportunities include:
- An unfulfilled customer need
- Inferior products or services currently available
- Arrival of new technologies
- Loosening of regulations
- Removal of international trade barriers
- Fluctuation in market pricing
- Cash surpluses

Threats
Changes in the external environmental also may present threats to your company and your industry. Some examples of such threats include:
- Shifts in consumer tastes away from your products
- Emergence of competitive companies and substitute products
- New regulations
- Increased trade barriers or barriers to entry
- Increases in costs
- Technology hacks

- Intellectual property infringement
- Lawsuits

The SWOT Matrix

A company should not necessarily pursue the more lucrative opportunities. Rather, it may have a better chance at developing a competitive advantage by identifying a fit between the company's strengths and upcoming opportunities. In some cases, the firm can overcome a weakness in order to prepare itself to pursue a compelling opportunity. To develop strategies that take into account the SWOT profile, a matrix of these factors can be constructed. The SWOT matrix (also known as a TOWS Matrix) is shown below:

	Strengths	**Weaknesses**
Opportunities	S – O Strategies	W – O Strategies
Threats	S – T Strategies	W – T Strategies

(Courtesy of QuickMBA)

S - O Strategies- pursue opportunities that are a good fit to the company's strengths

W - O Strategies- overcome weaknesses to pursue opportunities

S - T Strategies- identify ways your company can use its strengths to reduce its vulnerability to external threats

W – T Strategies- establish a defensive plan to prevent a company's weaknesses from making it highly susceptible to external threats

Appendix F - Home Office Shopping List

Furniture, Fixtures & Furnishings

- ☐ Desk
- ☐ Desk Chair
- ☐ Chair Seat Cushion
- ☐ Chair Mat
- ☐ File Cabinets
- ☐ Storage Cabinets
- ☐ Bookshelf
- ☐ Credenza/hutch
- ☐ Storage Boxes
- ☐ Trash Can
- ☐ Pictures
- ☐ Picture Frames
- ☐ Candy Bowl
- ☐ Key Rack
- ☐ Whiteboard
- ☐ Glassboard
- ☐ Corkboard
- ☐ Safe
- ☐ Chair Lumbar Support
- ☐ Door Hook
- ☐ Décor
- ☐ _____
- ☐ _____
- ☐ _____

Electronics & Peripherals

- ☐ Laptop Computer
- ☐ Laptop Stand
- ☐ Laptop Sleeve
- ☐ Laptop Carry Case
- ☐ Desktop Computer
- ☐ Internet Modem
- ☐ Desk Lamp
- ☐ Coffee Maker
- ☐ Mini Fridge
- ☐ Flash Drives
- ☐ CDs / CDRs
- ☐ Room Lights
- ☐ Phone System
- ☐ Software
- ☐ Small Fan
- ☐ Space Heater
- ☐ Air Purifier
- ☐ Wall Clock
- ☐ Shredder
- ☐ Calculator
- ☐ Headphones
- ☐ USB Hub
- ☐ USB Cables
- ☐ Music Player
- ☐ Flat screen Monitors
- ☐ 4-in-1 Office Machine
- ☐ External Hard Drive
- ☐ Wireless Keyboard
- ☐ Wireless Mouse
- ☐ Digital Camera
- ☐ Flat screen TV
- ☐ _____
- ☐ _____
- ☐ _____
- ☐ _____
- ☐ _____

Office Supplies

- ☐ Copy Paper
- ☐ Legal Pads
- ☐ Sticky Notes
- ☐ Push Pins
- ☐ Pens / Pencils
- ☐ Paper Clips
- ☐ Rubber Bands
- ☐ Stapler / Staples
- ☐ Hole Punch
- ☐ Pen Holder
- ☐ Staple Remover
- ☐ Candy / Snacks
- ☐ Coffee
- ☐ Batteries
- ☐ Flashlight
- ☐ Tape Measure
- ☐ Highlighters
- ☐ Scotch Tape
- ☐ Packaging Tape
- ☐ Light Bulbs
- ☐ Dry Erase Markers
- ☐ Whiteboard Eraser
- ☐ Ruler / Drawing Tools
- ☐ Office Machine Toner
- ☐ Business Card Holder
- ☐ Correction Tape
- ☐ Tool Set
- ☐ _____
- ☐ _____
- ☐ _____

Printing & Promotion

- ☐ Business Cards
- ☐ Brochures
- ☐ Postcards
- ☐ Rack cards
- ☐ Gift Certificates
- ☐ Loyalty Cards
- ☐ Banners
- ☐ Posters
- ☐ Yard Signs
- ☐ Menus
- ☐ Tents
- ☐ Envelopes
- ☐ Folders
- ☐ Decals
- ☐ Flyers
- ☐ Calendars
- ☐ Invitations
- ☐ Holiday Items
- ☐ Photo Items
- ☐ Phone Cases
- ☐ Cups and Mugs
- ☐ Mouse Pads
- ☐ Stickers
- ☐ Bookmarks
- ☐ Hang Tags
- ☐ Labels
- ☐ Letterhead
- ☐ Notepads
- ☐ Magnets
- ☐ Announcements
- ☐ Appointment Cards
- ☐ Branded Clothing
- ☐ Car Door Magnets
- ☐ Self-Inking Stamps
- ☐ Promotional Items
- ☐ Window Displays
- ☐ Bumper Stickers
- ☐ Binding Machine
- ☐ Business Checks
- ☐ _____
- ☐ _____
- ☐ _____

Appendix G – Testimonial Questionnaire

Why do you love (your business name)?
_____
_____
_____
_____
_____

Name: _____   **Date:** _____

Appendix H – Start-Up Checklist

- Office (professional office or home office)
    - ☐ Computer
    - ☐ Printer / Scanner
    - ☐ File cabinets
    - ☐ Organizers
    - ☐ Lighting
    - ☐ Artwork
    - ☐ Software
    - ☐ Desks
    - ☐ Chairs
    - ☐ Tables
    - ☐ Plants
    - ☐ Mini Fridge
    - ☐ Flat screen monitors
    - ☐ Credenza/hutch
    - ☐ Whiteboard
    - ☐ Coffee station
    - ☐ Office supplies

- Certifications
- Memberships and Subscriptions
- Legal Services
- Licenses
- Insurance
- Bond
- Printing
    - ☐ Letterhead
    - ☐ Coupons
    - ☐ Folders
    - ☐ Flyers
    - ☐ Tri-folds
    - ☐ Business cards
    - ☐ POP displays

- Website
- Leases - space and equipment (and security deposits)

Mark A. Torr

NOTES

Mark A. Torr

REFERENCES

10 Steps to Starting a Business. (2014, February 2). Retrieved from SBA.gov: http://www.sba.gov/content/follow-these-steps-starting-business

12 Reasons Why Keeping Good Records Benefits Your Business. (2011, December 6). Retrieved August 16, 2014, from NLDAccountancy.com: http://www.nldaccountancy.com/12-reasons-why-keeping-good-records-benefits-your-business/

20 Questions Before Starting. (2014, January 15). Retrieved from SBA.gov: http://www.sba.gov/content/20-questions-before-starting-business

(2014). Retrieved August 14, 2014, from RhymeZone.com: www.rhymezone.com

Angeles, S. (2013, December 24). *5 Simple Business Plan Templates for Entrepreneurs*. Retrieved from BusinessNewsDaily.com: http://www.businessnewsdaily.com/5680-simple-business-plan-templates.html

Beal, V. (2014). *Web 2.0.* Retrieved August 21, 2014, from Webopedia.com: http://www.webopedia.com/TERM/W/Web_2_point_0.html

Berry, T. (2013, September 6). *10 Business Plan Benefits You Might Be Forgetting.* Retrieved August 17, 2014, from Entrepreneur.com: http://www.entrepreneur.com/article/228220

Best Practice. (2009). Retrieved August 14, 2014, from InfoEntrepreneurs.com: http://www.infoentrepreneurs.org/en/guides/best-practice/

BrainyQuote Keywords. (2014, October). Retrieved from BrainyQuote: http://www.brainyquote.com/quotes/keywords.html

Brewster, P. (2007, September). Your Great Idea, Whose Time Has Come. *O Magazine*, p. 1 of 3. Retrieved from Oprah.com: http://www.oprah.com/omagazine/Your-Great-Idea-Whose-Time-Has-Come

Bughin, J. (2009, September). *How Companies are Benefitting From Web 2.0: McKinsey Global Survey Results.* Retrieved August 10, 2014, from McKinsey.com: http://www.mckinsey.com/insights/business_technology/how_companies_are_benefiting_from_web_20_mckinsey_global_survey_results

Business Structures. (2014, February 15). Retrieved from IRS.gov: http://www.irs.gov/Businesses/Small-Businesses-&-Self-Employed/Business-Structures

Checklist for Starting a Business. (2014, July 10). Retrieved from IRS.gov: http://www.irs.gov/Businesses/Small-Businesses-&-Self-Employed/Checklist-for-Starting-a-Business

Dalessandro, B. (2006, November 26). *Cost and Benefits of Taking Venture Capital Funding.* Retrieved August 19, 2014, from RebelCEO.com: http://rebelceo.com/vc-costs-and-benefits/

Date, R. (2012, February 2). *5 Ways to Manage Your Business' Social Media.* Retrieved July 16, 2014, from NFIB.com: http://www.nfib.com/article/5-ways-to-manage-your-business-social-media-59247/

Disclosure Statement. (n.d.). Retrieved August 16, 2014, from Investopedia.com: http://www.investopedia.com/terms/d/disclosurestatement.asp

Ebersole, J. G. (2013). *The Top Ten Benefits of an E-Newsletter, According to Your Strategic Thinking Business Coach.* Retrieved August 21, 2014, from EvanCarmichael.com: http://www.evancarmichael.com/Business-Coach/223/The-Top-Ten-Benefits-Of-An-ENewsletter-According-To-Your-Strategic-Thinking---Business-Coach.html

Eridon, C. (2013, November 6). *The Benefits of Blogging: Why Businesses Do It, and You Should Too.* Retrieved August 21, 2014, from HubSpot.com: http://blog.hubspot.com/marketing/the-benefits-of-business-blogging-ht

Financial Services. (2014, June 16). Retrieved from SBA.gov: http://www.sba.gov/content/financial-services

Helmenstine, A. M. (2014). *How Do Detergents Clean?* Retrieved August 20, 2014, from About.com: http://chemistry.about.com/od/howthingswork/f/detergentfaq.htm

Hoover, J. N. (2007, January 19). *The Problems With E-Mail.* Retrieved August 17, 2014, from InformationWeek.com: http://www.informationweek.com/the-problems-with-e-mail/d/d-id/1050876?

Is Entrepreneurship For You? (2014, March 2). Retrieved from SBA.gov: http://www.sba.gov/content/entrepreneurship-you

Julie. (2014). *A History of Business Cards.* Retrieved August 20, 2014, from Designer-Daily.com: http://www.designer-daily.com/a-history-of-business-cards-20266

Knutsen, J. (2014). *Improve Your Process - And Your Bottom Line - With Six Sigma.* Retrieved August 14, 2014, from Office.Microsoft.com: http://office.microsoft.com/en-us/visio-help/improve-your-process-and-your-bottom-line-with-six-sigma-HA001123336.aspx?CTT=5&origin=HA001165913

Leinhard, J. H. (2003). *Inventing Modern.* New York: Oxford University Press.

Littlefield, D. (2014, August 4). Restaurant's Bookkeeper Stole Millions. *Union Tribune San Diego.*

Mace, P. (2013, May 15). *Purpose of Disclosure Statements.* Retrieved August 16, 2014, from InsuranceLibrary.com: http://www.insurancelibrary.com/life-insurance/what-is-the-purpose-of-a-disclosure-statement-in-life-insurance-policies

Marketing Research Survey Templates. (2014). Retrieved August 17, 2014, from SurveyMonkey.com: https://www.surveymonkey.com/mp/market-research-survey-templates/

Mohamed, A. (2009, March). *A History of Cloud Computing.* Retrieved August 16, 2014, from ComputerWeekly.com: http://www.computerweekly.com/feature/A-history-of-cloud-computing

Neilson, K. (n.d.). *Top Ten Advantages of Using Online Storage Services.* Retrieved August 16, 2014, from Top 10 Reviews: http://online-storage-service-review.toptenreviews.com/top-ten-advantages-of-using-online-storage-services.html

O'Shaughnessy, E. (2014). *6 Reasons Giving Away Free Stuff Can Work for Your Small Business.* Retrieved August 12, 2014, from Ideas4SmallBiz: http://ideas4smallbiz.com/2012/04/6-reasons-giving-away-free-stuff-can-work-for-your-small-business/

Prive, T. (2012, November 27). *What Is Crowdfunding And How Does It Benefit The Economy?* Retrieved from Forbes.com: http://www.forbes.com/sites/tanyaprive/2012/11/27/what-is-crowdfunding-and-how-does-it-benefit-the-economy/

Recordkeeping. (2014, July 5). Retrieved from IRS.gov: http://www.irs.gov/Businesses/Small-Businesses-&-Self-Employed/Recordkeeping

SBA.gov. (2014, March 20). Retrieved from Managing Employees: http://www.sba.gov/content/managing-employees

See Color Theory in Action. (2014). Retrieved from Color-Wheel-Pro.com: http://www.color-wheel-pro.com/color-meaning.html

SWOT Analysis. (2010). Retrieved from QuickMBA.com: http://www.quickmba.com/strategy/swot/

The One Page Business Plan. (2008). Retrieved from Oprah.com: http://images.oprah.com/download/pdfs/omag/omag_200709_businessplan_consulting.pdf

The One-Page Business Plan. (n.d.). Retrieved from 100StartUp.com: http://100startup.com/resources/business-plan.pdf

The Story of Coffee. (2014). Retrieved August 17, 2014, from ICO.org: http://www.ico.org/coffee_story.asp

Vert, M. (2012, January 11). Terminology For Biorelated Polymers and Applications. *Pure Applied Chemistry*, pp. 377 - 410.

Wasserman, E. (2010, March 2). *The Pros and Cons of Setting Up a C Corp.* Retrieved August 20, 2014, from Inc.com: http://www.inc.com/guides/starting-a-c-corp.html

ABOUT THE AUTHOR

As you may have noticed by now, Mark is a breed all his own. Some may call his style unconventional, and the rest would probably agree! As Mark stated, he got his start as a business owner at a very young age. He was only 10 years old when he hit the streets with a bucket and some soap and began a weekly carwash service for his neighbors. That led to his first "real" job with a lawn maintenance company at age 14. Mark was a hard worker and passionate about everything.

One of Mark's mottos is, **"If it's worth doing, then it is worth overdoing."** While this is not the balanced approach he takes with his clients now, it might explain his "achiever" mindset in everything he does (see StrengthsFinder 2.0 reference in the book). As a kid, he would skateboard or bicycle about 10 miles a day. At 17 years old, he decided he was ready for some independence; he moved out and got his own apartment while he worked on finishing high school. Oh, and did Mark mention that he graduated Salutatorian of his high school class? That is second out of his entire class.

After high school, he did not slow down a bit. Mark put himself through college while working as a self-employed tile contractor. This allowed him to buy his first home when he was only 21 years old. While on a tile job, Mark was scouted to become a model and worked in Europe off and on for about 8 years. He was on television and on the cover and inside more magazines than I can count. Seeing him on billboards was fun but odd.

Following his time in Europe, he worked in sales and marketing with a new product development firm. Never one to let an opportunity pass him by, he left that lucrative position to earn his real estate license, become a loan officer, and travel with a real estate investment firm. Times were good... until they were not any longer and it was time for another change. The real estate market crashed and Mark decided it was time for one last ramp up. So he headed back to college with kids half his age to learn all about accounting, bookkeeping, and tax preparation. Mark graduated Summa Cum Laude with a degree in Accountancy.

And now you must be asking, "So what does Mark do for fun?" Well, I am glad you asked that. Aside from loving the fact that he is married to his best friend and business partner, he has the cutest daughter ever, and some of the most amazing (and tall) stepsons (there are three of them). Mark loves life. He loves traveling and photography. He cannot go more than a day or two without being in the ocean surfing. (Oh, and this is where I am supposed to write that the biggest wave he ever surfed was 22 feet high! It was down in Mexico and I was NOT a witness to this event. Sorry. Supposedly there was one eyewitness to this feat… but I don't really think that an old dog on the beach counts.) Mark loves to play tennis, or golf, or volleyball, or soccer, or ping pong, or pretty much any sport. Heck, he has even managed to make watching movies a sport. Ask him what a movie marathon is sometime. While he says he is not a big fan of reading, he still manages to spend about 1-2 hours a day reading *Surfer* magazine, the news online, trade publications, and his bible app. He works hard and plays hard, is abundantly humble, curiously intelligent, and savagely good-looking. He is well loved and adored by his fans.

~ Written by his most adoring fan, Mrs. Tiffany Torr

Author: **Mark A. Torr**

Photo by: Tehara Tweed Photography

You can learn more about Mark on his **LinkedIn** profile at:
https://www.linkedin.com/pub/mark-torr/5/8b/94a

Mark A. Torr

INDEX

99Designs.com- 99

A

ACT (by Sage)- 118
Adjust- 159, 166
Adjustment- 10
Adobe Acrobat- 118, 198
Advice- 2, 14, 15, 21, 81, 101
Advisors- 21, 44
Agreements- 8, 63, 194, 195
Amazon- 13, 34, 47, 61, 110, 118, 123
Ancillary products- 50, 62, 120
Anti-virus- 118, 119
Appointment- 7, 10, 120, 124, 137, 139, 183, 188
Appointment cards- 102, 124, 223
Apps- 7
Assets- 11, 12, 33, 39, 62, 63, 82-87
Assumptions- 18, 22, 35, 39, 131, 132, 191, 193
Attachment- 192, 193
Attributes- 8, 144, 180, 181

B

Beany Baby- 51
Behavior- 52, 128, 180, 183, 192, 193
Benchmarks- 11, 29, 41, 184-187
Benefits- 14, 37, 47, 79, 82, 125
Best practices- 179, 182-184, 191
Billing- 56, 159, 161, 170, 182
Bing- 145
Block schedule- 7, 110, 135, 152, 170
Blogging- 140, 142, 149-158
Bond- 43, 60
Bookkeeping- 2, 12, 154, 164, 169, 172-176

Books- 35, 95, 105, 165, 172, 174-176
Boston Tea Party- 30
Brand- 10, 28, 34, 45, 50, 57, 58, 68-70, 73, 74, 77, 78, 88, 95, 96, 102, 103, 109, 127, 128, 131, 139, 142, 146, 148-150, 166, 219
Branding- 57, 58, 71, 78, 95, 98, 99, 129, 143, 155
Brochure- 52, 98, 102, 124, 130, 223
Budget- 61, 62, 94, 110, 141, 171, 172, 218
Built-in content- 148
Business address- 79, 80, 89
Business cards- 12, 52, 58, 60, 78, 98, 100-102, 124, 129, 137, 223, 225
Business entity- 42, 43, 80, 81
Business expenses- 94, 95, 173
Business license- 3, 79, 81-86, 89, 90
Business lists- 129
Business model- 6, 10, 19, 40, 45, 50, 65, 67, 77, 78, 81, 91, 128, 132
Business name- 69, 70, 73, 80, 81, 84, 87, 88, 95, 96, 132, 137, 156
Business plan- 34, 37-40, 55, 64-66, 70, 107, 132, 144, 186, 216

C

Calculators- 148, 150, 151
Calendar- 7, 102, 124, 139, 163, 223
Capabilities- 33, 115, 131, 147, 148, 153, 182, 219
Capital- 37, 49, 62, 63, 65, 86, 168
Cash- 39, 63, 94, 95, 132, 159, 169, 174, 177, 220
Cash flow- 39, 46, 55, 61, 65, 66
C-Corporation- 42, 81, 82, 86, 87
Certificates- 49

Certifications- 27, 48, 60, 160, 172, 225
Chair- 19, 60, 111, 123, 222
Chamber of Commerce (COC)- 134
Changes- 59, 101, 103, 128, 187-191, 197, 201, 202
Character- 6-8, 153, 154, 164, 197
Checking account- 80, 81, 89, 91-95
Children- 3, 9, 109, 110, 117, 159, 161, 162, 170, 200
Choices- 26, 50, 51, 73, 74, 97, 111
Clients- 127, 128-130, 133, 135, 139, 140
Cloud storage- 120, 199-201
Color- 52, 59, 74, 95-99, 101, 183
Commitment- 13, 166, 168, 187, 197
Communication- 45, 46, 144, 185-191
Company name (see also Business name)- 52, 67-78, 81, 88, 219
Compensation- 44, 46
Competition- 53, 55, 192
Compliance- 86
Compliant- 49, 90, 195
Computer- 60, 106, 111, 112, 115
Concepts- 45, 96, 99, 202
Conditioning (behavior)- 52
Confidence- 4, 6, 56
Consequences- 9, 112, 175
Consult- 148, 176
Consultant- 192, 193
Continuing Professional Education (CPE)- 27, 172
Contracts- 45, 167, 168, 194, 195
Contributions- 11, 46, 190
Corrections- 38, 39
Cost analysis- 14
Costco- 19, 48, 120, 166
Craigslist- 61, 98, 99, 110, 111, 118, 129
Creation- 29
Credit card- 93, 95, 167-169, 177
Crowdfunding- 64
Customizing- 131, 142

D

Database- 118, 120, 132, 162, 191
Day job- 14, 159, 161
Debit card- 94, 169
Decision makers- 43, 63, 65
Decision making- 20
Decisions- 12, 15, 17-21, 43, 45, 65, 81, 94, 115, 159, 160, 181, 183, 205
Delegating- 38
Depreciation- 62
Desk- 60, 62, 105, 106, 109-111, 111-113, 115-117, 120, 123
Desktop computer- 117, 123, 222
Determination- 6
Digital files- 198, 199
Direct sales- 1
Discipline- 8
Disclaimers- 43, 76, 194, 203
Disclosures- 194-196
Discount pricing- 56, 129
Discounts- 59, 129, 130, 160, 165, 168
Distractions- 106
Domain name- 88, 141, 144
Draws- 46
Dreamers- 12, 27

E

eBay- 61, 110
Economics- 192
Economy- 5, 192
Educated guess- 38, 39
Efficiencies- 131, 179
Efficiency- 19, 36, 109, 140, 179, 181, 182, 186, 189-191
Efficient- 9, 109, 179, 181, 183
Electronics- 123, 222
Emotions- 15, 17, 25, 73, 99, 192, 193
Employee- 8, 14, 43-46, 50, 83-86, 146, 186, 187, 205

Employer Identification Number (EIN)- 80, 88
Energy- 6, 9, 11, 20, 93, 106, 166
Ethics- 6
Excel- see Microsoft Excel
Executive suites- 125
Executive summary- 37, 40
Exit strategy- 34, 217
Expense accounts- 172
Expenses- 2, 39, 46, 65, 78, 86, 91, 94, 95, 134, 135, 149, 159, 160, 171, 173, 174, 179, 197

F

Facebook- 143, 152-155, 165, 183
Facility- 49, 199
Facts- 15, 18-20, 22, 156, 159, 181, 183
Family members- 8, 9, 63, 85, 107-110, 120, 133, 161, 170
Features- 47, 92, 118, 119, 122, 142, 144, 148, 190
Feelings- 15, 20, 66, 95
Fictitious Business Name (FBN)- 79, 81, 83-86, 89
Filing baskets- 198
File cabinet- 60, 109, 112, 114, 123, 199
File maintenance- 197
File sharing- 146-148
Finances- 43, 59, 81, 170
Financial planning- 185
Financial statements- 66, 173, 175, 197
Fine print- 195, 196
Firewall- 118, 119, 191
Fixtures- 110, 123, 222
Fonts- 52, 95, 97, 196
Forecasting- 185
Form 1040- 42, 82, 83, 143
Form 1099-Misc- 44, 88
Form Schedule-C- 42, 78, 82, 83, 88, 90
Form SS-4- 89

Form W-2- 46, 83, 84, 86
Forums- 155
Fry's Electronics- 120
Full-service- 50, 59
Furniture- 15, 28, 61, 105, 110, 120, 123, 205, 222
Future- 18, 28, 29, 39, 41, 42, 51, 53, 135, 161, 167, 175, 186

G

GAAP- 18
George Chapman- 21
Goals- 9, 12, 39, 41, 49, 57, 184, 216
Google- 87, 96, 141, 145, 179
Google calendar- 7
Google drive- 147, 199
Government entities- 49
Government oversight- 49
Government regulation- 48, 49
Graphic artist- 98-100
Groups- 129, 133-136, 152-156

H

Hardware- 115, 120
Health insurance- 6
Hobbies- 3, 26
Hobbyists- 1, 90
Hobby- 2, 3, 22, 26, 207
Home-based- 24, 79, 211
Home occupation permit- 89
Home office- 49, 60, 105-114, 118, 121-123, 125, 160, 167, 222
Homemaker- 2
Hoovers.com- 133
Hosting sites- 142
House- 3, 9, 52, 105, 107-111, 115, 117, 120, 121, 160, 192

I

Ikea- 61, 111
Image- 50, 70, 98, 99, 103, 108, 125
Impact- 17, 25, 41, 45, 53, 68, 70, 107, 160, 183, 210
Income streams- 78
Independent contracting- 1, 44
Information Technology (IT)- 190
Innovation- 122, 184, 198, 190
Insurance- 43, 44, 48, 60, 196, 205
Insurance benefits- 15
IRS- 2, 3, 18, 19, 44, 45, 82-84, 86-90

J

Judgment- 35, 135, 156, 157

K

Knowledge- 18, 20, 21, 92, 144, 172, 186, 219

L

Laptop- 116, 117, 120, 122, 123, 161, 222
Leadership- 185
Leads clubs- 134
Learning curve- 26, 34, 50, 144, 166, 183
Leases- 61, 125, 225
Legal- 2, 19, 42, 44, 46, 60, 76, 81, 88, 105, 225
LEGOLAND- 162
Lessons- 12, 35, 75
Letters of engagement- 194
Liability- 18, 28, 42-45, 48, 79, 81-85, 87, 90, 203, 219, 220
License- see Business license
Lighting- 60, 112, 132
Limitations- 1, 12, 48, 154
Limited Liability Company (LLC)- 42, 81, 82
LinkedIn- 44, 153, 154
Loans- 37, 64, 65, 71, 93, 168

Local market- 53, 54
Location- 34, 36, 40, 41, 49, 90, 93, 107, 112, 113, 125, 130, 166, 167, 199, 201
Logo- 31, 34, 57, 58, 67-69, 95-101
Long-term- 6, 33, 49, 162, 167, 168, 192
Loss leader- 161-163, 165

M

Mailing lists- 132, 133, 189
Management- 6, 9, 38, 42, 44, 118, 140, 142, 154, 175, 180, 184-188, 190, 192, 198
Manager(s)- 8, 13, 35, 45, 93, 94
Marketing- 1, 2, 27, 38, 41, 44, 47, 51, 57, 70, 84, 95, 127, 129, 133, 149, 152, 183, 188-190, 216, 217
Marketplace- 5, 47, 174
Meeting(s)- 9, 25, 86, 110, 113, 134, 136, 182
Micromanage- 6
Microsoft Excel- 53, 59, 95, 118, 171
Microsoft Office- 118, 141
Microsoft PowerPoint- 52, 118, 155
Microsoft Word- 25, 59, 97, 114, 118, 198
Mileage- 151, 170, 171, 177
MileBug.com- 170, 171
Mission Statement- 41, 47, 67
Mistakes- 12, 58, 134, 173, 202
Momentum- 8, 30, 144, 148, 161
Money- 3, 4, 11, 12, 18, 19, 24, 46, 51, 52, 62-64, 90, 94, 121, 122, 141, 142, 145, 146, 149, 160, 170, 173, 175, 183, 212
Morals- 6
Motivation- 6, 7
Multi-level marketing- 1, 2

N

Name- see Business name
Name search- 78, 87
Negative- 9, 21, 23, 45, 51, 70, 71, 95, 164, 166, 177, 183, 208

Newsletter- 146, 148, 149, 188
Niche- 77, 130
Non-profit activities- 1

O

Objections- 21
Office supplies- 19, 60, 124, 223, 225
Off-site storage- 199
Operations- 49, 151, 170, 179, 187, 192, 193
Opinions- 21, 99, 131, 156
Opportunities- 1, 33, 35, 53, 66, 114, 143, 202, 219-221
Organizations- 91, 133-135, 155, 156, 188, 190, 199
Overstock.com- 61

P

Partnership(s) and LLPs- 81, 83, 85, 91, 198
Payment(s)- 44, 82-84, 87, 95, 140, 148, 168-170, 197, 198
PayPal- 93, 167-169
Performance- 180, 181, 185-187, 194
Permits- 49, 90
Personal expenses- 94, 95
Perspective- 35, 56, 198
Pessimist- 21
Pet Rock- 51
Philosophy- 5, 41, 47, 55, 140, 149, 180, 192, 202
PO Box- 79
Policies- 45, 139, 186, 194, 196
Policy- 43, 45, 59, 73, 78, 93, 186
Portals- 146, 147
Positive- 1, 6, 9, 21, 25, 45, 64, 130, 139, 157, 162, 164, 166, 183
Posting- 129, 150, 152-156, 158, 183
PowerPoint- see Microsoft PowerPoint
Preference- 98, 109, 181
Presentations- 52, 135, 136, 157

Price- 32, 52, 53, 56, 57, 62, 80, 92, 118, 122, 123, 129-131, 147, 160, 161, 165, 190, 214
Price point- 53, 56, 129, 131
Printing- 60, 97-102, 114, 118, 124, 149, 165, 168, 223, 225
Priorities- 38
Priority- 13
Privacy- 108, 117, 119, 195
Product(s)- 102, 129, 139, 161, 162, 181, 188-190
Proficiency- 26
Protocol- 44, 93, 113, 190
Public speaking- 6, 135, 155, 156

Q

Quality- 36, 48, 52, 70, 150, 155, 164, 180-188
Quality of life- 11
Quit- 14, 99, 127

R

Ralph Waldo Emerson- 52
Ramp-up- 26, 28, 30, 34, 161
Rates- 132, 149, 159-161, 171
Realistic- 6, 29, 62, 66, 106, 159, 185
Reconcile- 46, 62
Records- 171, 177, 197
ReferenceUSA.com- 54, 132
Referrals- 133, 154, 216
Regulation- 19, 46, 48, 49, 90, 220
Relocate- 14, 24, 28, 211
Reminders- 7, 37, 188
Rent- 1, 40, 55, 160, 163, 172
Rental property- 1
Research- 19, 26, 27, 53, 56, 65, 140, 146, 148, 152, 156
Resources- 11, 12, 51, 64, 65, 132, 159, 176, 180, 182, 219
Results- 11, 17, 22, 25, 38, 39, 53, 69, 79, 87,

91, 100, 101, 125, 132, 134, 139, 145, 146, 164, 165, 180-183, 187
Resume- 44, 153
Revenues- 41, 46, 49, 62, 63, 65, 90, 94, 103, 125, 128, 159-161, 176, 179
Rotary Club- 134, 135

S

Sales- 1, 2, 13, 20, 28, 38, 39, 61, 65, 90, 91, 131, 132, 136, 148, 168, 180, 183, 185, 188, 192, 217
Sales tax- 28, 90, 91
Sales tax license- 90, 91
Salespeople- 20, 131
Savvy- 6, 8, 56
Schedule (see also Block schedule)- 7, 8, 10, 38, 120, 135, 188, 198
S-Corporation- 42, 78, 80-84, 86-89
Search engine- 53, 87, 91, 139, 144-146, 149
Search Engine Optimization (SEO)- 145
Secrets- 17, 46, 47
Security- 42, 61, 79, 93, 118, 188, 191, 193, 197, 200, 225
Self-starter- 6
Seller's permit- 90, 91
Service Corps of Retired Executives (SCORE)- 39
Services provided- 41, 47
Shopping- 19, 92, 123, 222
Shopping strip (center)- 36, 160
Short-term- 29, 33, 49, 67, 78, 146, 162
Six Sigma- 179-182
Skillset- 5, 7, 15, 26, 40, 153, 205
Skype- 116, 122
Small business owner- 1-6, 40, 49, 82, 86, 90, 105, 107, 173, 174, 191
Small Business Administration (SBA)- 37, 64, 65
Small Business Development Center (SBDC)- 39

SmartFax- 121, 122
Social media- 31, 59, 75, 139, 152-156
Social networks- 152
Society- 8
Software- 7, 60, 62, 115-120, 123, 177, 191
Sole proprietor- 42, 43, 46, 81, 83, 85, 88-90, 220
Solutions- 21, 47, 158, 216
Source documents- 177
Specialized- 48, 50, 131, 132
Specialties- 12
Specialty- 111
Sphere of influence- 44, 151
Spouse- 9, 13, 161
Spreadsheet- 25, 53, 54, 62, 95, 160, 171, 183
Square- see The Square
Staff- 23, 35, 41, 73, 86, 89, 162, 185-187, 191-193, 209, 219
Staffing- 44
Stakeholders- 37, 41, 45, 46, 65, 66, 84, 92, 190
Standards- 184, 188
Start-up costs (expenses)- 11, 59, 62, 160, 208
Storage- 25, 109, 112-115, 123, 199-201
Store front- 13, 23, 24, 36, 80
Strategic planning- 185
Strategy- 29, 34, 37, 38, 67, 73, 94, 108, 137, 159, 161-163, 174, 179, 183, 185, 217
Strengths- 8, 12, 37, 53, 197, 219, 221
StrengthsFinder 2.0- 7, 8, 26,
Studio- 13, 34, 54, 105, 128, 160
Sub-contractors- 44, 89
Sub-name- 69, 72, 73
Supervisors- 35
Survey(s)- 31, 205, 213
Sweet spot- 29, 179, 184
Swiper (card)- 167-169
SWOT analysis- 53, 219, 221

T

Task(s)- 7, 38, 44, 110, 161, 172
Taxes- 12, 44, 81, 84, 86, 91, 122, 154, 168, 172-174, 198
Tax advantages- 2
Tax benefits- 2, 28, 172
Tax ID number- 89
Tax payments- 82-84, 87, 197, 198
Tax return- 2, 10, 42, 62, 78, 82-86, 88, 163, 169, 177
Tax returns- 162, 172-175, 182
Technician- 35
Templates- 26, 31, 39, 45, 72, 141, 142, 145, 148-150
Terms of use- 194
Testimonials- 130, 139, 224
Text blasts- 188
Texting- 188
The E-Myth- 34, 35
The Square- 168
Theories- 22
Theory- 31
Time management- 9, 140
Tolerance- 109, 160
Tools- 7, 8, 12, 15, 17, 22, 26, 28, 48, 59, 77, 92, 96, 97, 101, 110, 118, 124, 144-146, 150, 152, 154, 155, 167, 180, 181, 185, 186, 198, 205, 223
Track- 38, 62, 94, 151, 156, 170, 171, 183
Tracking- 38, 39, 94, 155, 170, 183, 187, 201
Training- 15, 165, 172, 186, 187, 205
Trends- 27, 53, 75, 128, 152, 174
Twitter- 153-155

U

UPS Store- 79
Use tax- 90
Utilities- 172

V

Vacation- 9
Value- 14, 39, 46, 47, 52, 56, 57, 62, 125, 127, 146, 147, 155, 158, 162, 163, 187
Venture capital (VC)- 37, 62
Vision- 1, 27, 30, 95, 99, 217
Visionaries- 12, 27
Visionary- 27
Vistaprint.com- 96, 100, 101, 103
Voice-over IP- 122
Vonage- 122

W

Weaknesses- 8, 37, 53, 197, 219-221
Web 2.0- 152
Web links- 151, 152, 203
Websites- 52, 96, 97, 117, 133, 139, 141, 150, 151, 188, 189, 203
Website templates- 141, 142, 148-151
William Lyon Phelps- 22
WinCleaner- 118, 119
Winston Churchill- 6, 57
Worker- 8, 35, 44, 119, 196
Workspace- 12, 106

Y

Yahoo- 145
Year-end- 44, 46, 174, 175, 177, 197
Year-end statements- 177
Yellow Pages- 53
YouTube- 154, 155

(thank you)

Made in the USA
Middletown, DE
08 May 2019